UNHOLY MADNESS

The Church's Surrender to Psychiatry

SETH FARBER

InterVarsity Press
Downers Grove, Illinois

InterVarsity Press
P.O. Box 1400, Downers Grove, IL 60515
World Wide Web: www.ivpress.com
E-mail: mail@ivpress.com

InterVarsity Press® is the book-publishing division of InterVarsity Christian Fellowship/USA®, a student movement active on campus at hundreds of universities, colleges and schools of nursing in the United States of America, and a member movement of the International Fellowship of Evangelical Students. For information about local and regional activities, write Public Relations Dept., InterVarsity Christian Fellowship/USA, 6400 Schroeder Rd., P.O. Box 7895, Madison, WI 53707-7895.

ISBN 0-8308-1939-8

Printed in the United States of America ♻

Library of Congress Cataloging-in-Publication Data

Farber, Seth, 1951-
   Unholy madness : the church's surrender to psychiatry / Seth
Farber.
      p.   cm.
   Includes bibliographical references.
   ISBN 0-8308-1939-8 (pbk. : alk. paper)
   1. Psychiatry and religion.   2. Christianity—Psychology.
I. Title.
BT732.4.F37   1999
261.5'15—dc21   99-21613
                                                                                    CIP

| 21 | 20 | 19 | 18 | 17 | 16 | 15 | 14 | 13 | 12 | 11 | 10 | 9 | 8 | 7 | 6 | 5 | 4 | 3 | 2 | 1 |
| 16 | 15 | 14 | 13 | 12 | 11 | 10 | 09 | 08 | 07 | 06 | 05 | 04 | 03 | 02 | 01 | 00 | 99 | | | |

In tribute to Thomas Szasz
and to R. D. Laing (1926-1989),
intellectual pioneers,
citizens who renounced the world
of master and slave.

Contents

Acknowledgments

I am indebted to Rodney Clapp for his faith in this project, his consistency of focus and his firm editorial guidance.

For the kind of spiritual and emotional support that makes this kind of endeavor possible, I am grateful to my parents, Hardina Dahl, Patricia Farber Martinez, Justin and Miranda, Father David Kossey, Bishop Seraphim Sigrist, Danielle Deschamps, Deniz Tekiner, Ray Russ, Larry Simon, John Rempel, the Gallup twins, Jack Felder, Trevor Grant, Mitchell Hoag, Ron Goldman, James Mancuso, Pasquale Galante, Leonard Frank, George Ebert, Rita DiCarlo, Frank Schaeffer, Laura Woodruff, Jerry Foley, Evelyn Woodsom, Harold Channer and Monty Weinstein.

In addition to the intellectual influences cited in these pages, I am indebted to Sri Aurobindo.

Introduction

This book is the product of over twenty years of study in the field of psychology. Had I read a book with a similar perspective when I first began graduate study in psychology in 1976, I probably would have dismissed it as an exaggeration or as unduly cynical. Although my assessment of the mental health professions is highly critical, I am, of course, not unaware that many persons have had positive experiences with psychotherapists. I know that because of this fact and because of the popularity of psychology in modern society—of its ideological hegemony—many readers will find my conclusions difficult to accept. Some will find them offensive.

I ask my readers only to consider my ideas carefully and to bear in mind that I was once a true believer in the power of the mental health professions to act as a redemptive force in a society in crisis. I was aware of abuses, but I thought them remediable. I did not come to my current position easily. It was a slow and arduous process of disillusionment that led finally to the repudiation of my most cherished beliefs about the profession of which I had chosen to become a member.

Maintaining this position has not been painless either. My views have not made me popular among my colleagues and have led to the foreclosure of many opportunities for professional advancement. Yet I cannot—or will not—be silent or more "diplomatic." I believe that I am acting in accord with God's will. This belief has been strengthened over the years through my encounters with remarkable persons, both mental health professionals and former "mental patients," who took risks and made sacrifices in order to defend the victims and potential victims of the mental health system.

I did not know when I first became a Christian that the development of my understanding of the meaning and implications of my Christian faith would eventually lead me to a crossroads where I would have to choose between two masters—between the mental health professions and Christianity, between the mental health *religion* and Jesus Christ. But this is what has occurred, and I have made my choice. This book is an appeal to the church to affirm its own identity as the body of Christ—the medium for the growth of Christians, the crucible for the creation of a new humanity —and to recognize the mental health system as a rival religion, a crude form of idolatry inimical to the dissemination of the Christian faith and to the realization of the Christian vision of the kingdom of God on earth.

The church's surrender to psychiatry has been facilitated by its tendency to subject human life to an artificial compartmentalization: private versus public, spiritual versus political, otherworldly versus worldly. For too long the church has claimed the private, the spiritual and the otherworldly as its proper domain while allowing secular authorities to dominate the public, the political and the worldly. This strange division of authority stems historically, I argue in chapters four and six, from the church's original decision in the fourth and fifth centuries to accommodate the Christian mission to worldly power and to accept a collaboration with the Roman emperor Constantine.

Since the rise of modern psychology/psychiatry there has been yet a new compartmentalization: the spiritual versus the psychological. But there are no "psychological" needs or capacities that are not spiritual. By accepting this spurious bifurcation of the spiritual into the (secular) psychological and the (nonsecular) spiritual, the church has severely compromised its authority and enabled the practitioners of the idolatrous religion of mental health to promulgate their faith system and thus to gain control over the hearts and minds (and pocketbooks) of millions of Americans. I have attempted throughout this book to demonstrate that the rationale for this usurpation of power by the mental health professions and for the abdication of responsibility by the church is specious: mental health professionals do not possess highly specialized "scientific expertise" enabling them to uniquely minister to individuals' "psychological" needs.

Those who sanction this division of life into the secular and religious spheres would do well to heed the words of Father Georges Florovsky:

Christianity is not an individualistic religion and it is not only concerned for the salvation of the soul. Christianity is the Church, i.e., a Community, the New People of God, leading its corporate life according to its peculiar principles. And this life cannot be split into departments, some of which might have been ruled by any other and heterogeneous principles. Spiritual leadership of the Church can hardly be reduced to an occasional guidance given to individuals or groups living under conditions utterly uncongenial to the Church. The legitimacy of those conditions must be questioned first of all. The task of a complete re-creation or re-shaping of the whole fabric of human life cannot or must not be avoided or declined. One can not serve two Masters and a double allegiance is a poor solution.[1]

As I have already implied, my conclusions about psychology were not reached in an ivory tower. They emerged in the process of interacting—as therapist, advocate and friend—with individuals deemed "mentally ill" and studying with some of the leading innovators in and critics of the mental health system. Thus it seemed appropriate to begin the book (chapter one) by revealing some of the formative experiences in my transformation from a mental health true believer to a mental health heretic, with the hope of arousing readers' doubts about some of the culturally entrenched dogmas about the "mentally ill."

In chapter two I document the alarming extent to which mental health professionals have colonized domains of human life that used to be under the authority of the family, school or community. I have also exposed the unethical—and frequently illegal—practices the mental health professions have resorted to in order to expand their markets. To a large degree the prophecies of George Orwell and Aldous Huxley have come true.

In chapter three I examine the arguments of two prominent dissident psychiatrists, Thomas Szasz and R. D. Laing, and attempt to demonstrate that they are heirs of the Christian revolution. Revealing that society fails to embody Christian and democratic values,[2] they render problematic psychology's reification and promotion of adjustment as the norm and criteria of "mental health," and as an absolute value to be accepted and sanctioned by religious and secular alike.

R. D. Laing and Thomas Szasz were not merely critics of psychiatry but also protagonists in a battle for democracy that actually began with the ministry of Jesus Christ centuries ago. I appeal to the church to act as an agent of democratization and to challenge new modes of domination undergirded by the ideology of "professional expertise."

Chapter four is an argument for a non-Constantinian interpretation of Christianity. In this chapter I explicate the eschatological, political and this-worldly dimensions of the Christian faith, demonstrating that the spiritualist interpretation of Christianity is inconsistent both with Scripture and with the practice of the early church before its alliance with Constantine.

In chapter five I attempt to demonstrate that the concept of mental illness is not "scientific," not "value-neutral," but the reflection of a misanthropic anthropology first elaborated by Augustine in the fifth century (in his book *The City of God*). I call upon Christians to repudiate this anthropology and to reaffirm the biblical vision, which is, I argue, humanistic in its essence. It is appropriate here to quote Jean Delumeau, the French scholar who has documented so powerfully how the most grim version of Augustinianism became dominant in Europe in the thirteenth to eighteenth centuries:

> Augustinism . . . could only have brought on fears among both the instructors and pupils of the church (or at least among the most motivated of these people). In any case, the result was a type of preaching that spoke more of the Passion of the Savior than of His Resurrection, more of sin than of pardon, of the Judge than of the Father, of Hell than of Paradise. There was thus a true deviation from St. Paul's tidings that 'Where sin abounded, grace did much more abound' (Rom. 5:20). Hence one might consider whether the rejection of an oppressive doctrinal campaign was one of the causes of the 'de-Christianization' of the West.[3]

It is a time for a renaissance of Christianity—of Christian humanism.

The argument that the church is—or ought to be—a counterculture based on values antithetical to this world and to the mental health system is the focus of chapter six. I criticize Christians for credulously accepting the positivistic scientific-expertise claims of the mental health professions, for failing to scrutinize the philosophical premises on which various psychologies have been based (as revealed in chapter five) and for capitulating to the mental health system.

Chapter six, as well as this book as a whole, is influenced by my reading of neo-Anabaptist theologians (and to some degree Eastern Orthodox theologians) who have argued that Christians have become enmeshed in and co-opted by power structures they originally entered with the hopes of transforming. (This is precisely what has occurred with the "Christian psychology" movement.) Thomas Finger wrote, "In our view . . . the Church impacts this world not chiefly by seeking to help its present structures to function better, but by presenting it with new alternative possibilities."[4] This is what the church must do today if it is to become once again a viable instrument for spiritual and social change.

In chapter seven I attempt to demonstrate that the "mentally ill" are by and large victims of processes of professional stigmatization and social exclusion. Thus the "chronicity" of schizophrenia is largely an artifact of the "treatments" of the mental health system. I also argue that emotional breakdowns and "schizophrenic episodes" are frequently initiatory experiences that present the individual (given the proper environment) with an opportunity to be reborn in the Spirit as a disciple of Christ.

The concluding chapter makes specific suggestions for restoring the authority of the church. It is a call for the church to recognize new modes of domination (disguised by the ideology of professionalism) and to become, as it has been in the past, a force for social reconstruction (democratization) and spiritual regeneration.

1

The Religion of Psychiatry

The symbol that most specifically characterizes psychiatrists as members of a distinct group of doctors is the concept of schizophrenia; and the ritual that does so most clearly is their diagnosing this disease in persons who do not want to be their patients. . . .

Schizophrenia has become the Christ on the cross that psychiatrists worship, and in whose name they march in the battle to reconquer reason from unreason, sanity from insanity; reverence toward it has become the mark of psychiatric orthodoxy, and irreverence toward it the mark of psychiatric heresy.
THOMAS SZASZ, *SCHIZOPHRENIA*

Mental illness is a myth whose function is to disguise and thus render more palatable the bitter pill of moral conflicts in human relations. In asserting that there is no such thing as mental illness, I do not deny that people have problems coping with life and each other.
THOMAS SZASZ, *THE UNTAMED TONGUE*

The two most prominent critics of the concept of mental illness during the time that I was in high school, college and later in graduate school were psychiatrists Thomas Szasz and R. D. Laing. Their period of greatest renown was in the "countercultural" 1960s, when even in the mental health professions there was an openness to considering new ideas. Although Szasz stressed his philosophical differences with Laing (see below), they were almost always viewed by most of their readers as being in the same camp. Although I was initially very sympathetic to their ideas, it was not until I decided to become a psychologist in 1976 that I studied their argument more carefully. Two years after I had completed graduate school, I reached the conclusion that they were correct: mental illness does not exist. I do not believe that mad people—for example, persons who hear voices or think strange things like the TV set is talking to them—are "mentally ill" or "schizophrenic." I do not believe they suffer from a medical condition optimally treated by psychiatrists. My heresy eventually led me in 1987 to make contact with and later support what was then known as the "mental patients liberation movement." I will recount here some of the books and experiences that contributed to my rejection of the essential tenets of psychiatric orthodoxy.

The Psychiatric Heretics
In 1961 psychiatrist Thomas Szasz's seminal book *The Myth of Mental Illness*[1] attempted to demonstrate a challenging idea: Mental illnesses do not exist. In principle it is impossible for the mind, an immaterial entity, to be afflicted by an illness. Undoubtedly there could be genuine physical illnesses that caused mental symptoms, but Szasz maintained (and still does today) that this is almost never the case with the phenomena designated as *mental illness*. The term *mental illness* is a demeaning label applied by psychiatrists to persons whose behavior they disapprove of, a label used to justify controlling these persons under the guise of "treating" their illnesses. Szasz did not deny that individuals deemed mentally ill were suffering, but he insisted that what they were suffering from were not illnesses but "problems in living."[2]

Szasz argued that the myth of mental illness entailed its corollary, that life would be harmonious and social intercourse would be entirely satisfying if it were not for the disruptive influence of mental illness. This obscured the fact that for most people life is "a continuous struggle, not for biological survival but for a 'place in the sun,' 'peace of mind,' or some other meaning or value." Happiness, Szasz argued, is the exception rather than the norm. Human beings are constantly faced with ethical, personal and social conflicts, with "problems in living," whether these are biological, economic, political or sociopsychological in nature. The myth of mental illness serves only to obfuscate the existence of these conflicts and thus forestalls tackling and overcoming these problems.[3]

The force of Szasz's argument was strengthened by the fact that he was a psychiatrist himself. He was not an outsider who could be accused of not understanding the profession, of lacking the knowledge required to understand the intricacies of the human psyche. He was an insider who had risen to the highest ranks within his own profession and then renounced the very dogma that defined the profession. It was as if a cardinal in the Catholic Church were to announce that Christ was not divine. In short, Szasz was a heretic, a church member who holds beliefs opposed to church dogma.

Why did Szasz pit himself against his own profession? Certainly not out of self-interest, at least not in any narrow sense of the term. It was because moral values that Szasz held sacred—liberty, autonomy, responsibility and human dignity—were being violated by psychiatry. He was also motivated by compassion for the outsiders, the aliens, the deviants, for those who became the scapegoats of society and psychiatry. Szasz's readiness to subordinate self-interest to principle did not earn him the respect of most other professionals. Some even saw it as proof that he was himself mentally imbalanced. I remember reading the remark of one psychiatrist, "It's a sick bird that fouls its own nest."

To term Szasz a heretic is to imply that the mental health system has for many reasons replaced the church as the arbiter of ultimate values and meaning, a point Szasz has made repeatedly. He stated that in premodern societies individuals derived their sense of legitimacy from God, whereas in modern society they derive it from science. Accordingly, the psychiatrist has replaced the priest as a guardian of society's moral and spiritual values, and as the judge of what or who is deserving of praise or blame, esteem or condemnation, compassion or contempt, reverence or pity.

Several years after Thomas Szasz's book appeared, R. D. Laing's second book, *The Politics of Experience*, was published. This made him an instant celebrity on college campuses around the country, a symbol for a generation in revolt against the ways of the past. In this book Laing wrote,

> The condition of alienation, of being asleep, of being unconscious, is the condition of the normal man. Society highly values its normal man. It educates children to lose themselves and to become absurd, and thus to be normal. Normal men have killed perhaps a hundred million of their fellow men in the last fifty years. . . . Our society may itself have become biologically dysfunctional, and some forms of schizophrenia may have a socio-biological function that we have not yet recognized.[4]

Laing and Szasz did not merely denounce the abuses of psychiatry, but they claimed that psychiatry in its present form was intrinsically abusive, merely one grotesque symptom of an unjust society where the strong and the powerful enrich themselves at the expense of the weak and the vulnerable while masquerading as their benefactors, their doctors, their saviors. Szasz wrote, "The labelling of persons as mentally healthy or diseased [by psychiatrists] . . . constitutes the initial act of validation and invalidation, pronounced by the high priest of modern scientific religion, the psychiatrist; it justifies the expulsion of the sacrificial scapegoat, the mental patient, from the community."[5] Or as Laing put it,

> The person labelled is inaugurated not only into a role, but into a career of patient, by the concerted action of a coalition (a "conspiracy"), of family, G.P., mental health officer, psychiatrist, nurses, psychiatric social workers, and often fellow patients. The "committed" person labelled as patient, and specifically as "schizophrenic," is degraded from full existential and legal status as human agent and responsible person to someone no longer in possession of his own definition of himself. . . . After being subjected to a degradation ceremonial [sic] known as psychiatric examination, he is bereft of his civil liberties in being imprisoned in the total institution known as a "mental" hospital. More completely, more radically than anywhere else in our society, he is invalidated as a human being.[6]

My Training as a Psychologist and Retraining as a Family Therapist

When I was twenty-four, I decided to become a psychologist, and I entered graduate school a year later, in 1976. Despite the fact that I had read and been influenced by Szasz and Laing, as I progressed through graduate school I became more and more influenced by the psychoanalytic (Freudian) way of looking at the world. Secretly I thought of myself as an initiate into the great Freudian tradition; my readings and studies had given me insight into the complexities of the human psyche, and I possessed the esoteric knowledge that would enable me to heal my patients and to guide them through the spiritual labyrinth of the world. I had succumbed to the intellectual glamour of the Freudian worldview. The influence of Laing and Szasz had waned, although there was at least a residuum of my former heresy: unlike most psychoanalysts, I believed that "schizophrenia" was a curable, rather than an incurable, emotional disorder—and I found "schizophrenics" to be fascinating people.

Fortunately, after graduate school I gradually became disenchanted with Freudianism (psychoanalysis). I attribute this disenthrallment initially to my study of family therapy, which convinced me once again that there was no such entity as "mental illness" and that the person deemed mentally ill by mental health authorities was being scapegoated for problems whose locus was not *within* the individual but *between* individuals, usually within the family.

In other words, the model of family therapy that I studied maintained that the cause of the present distress of the "identified patient"[7] was not so much traumatic events in the past but dysfunctional relationships in the present. The solution therefore was not, as Freudianism insisted, to relive the past and attempt to achieve insight into the origins of one's problems but to modify the dynamics of interpersonal relationships involving the "patient" in the present.

In 1985 I studied with psychiatrist Salvador Minuchin, one of the original founders of the family therapy movement, author of numerous books and an international authority on family therapy. The following year I studied with Jay Haley, another family therapy luminary, who had previously worked with Minuchin at the Philadelphia Child Guidance Center. Both Haley and Minuchin became renowned for the extraordinary effectiveness of their family therapy interventions on the lives of individuals regarded by psychoanalysts as "severely mentally ill."[8] (In the 1950s when Haley and Minuchin were first establishing themselves are professionals, psychoanalysis was the dominant form of treatment in the mental health field, and they encountered considerable opposition in their efforts to promote family therapy as a more effective alternative.)

Haley explicitly rejected the idea that "schizophrenia" was a disease, and he described his successful treatment of "disturbed young people" in his book *Leaving Home*,[9] which was published in 1980. Haley's theory was that the young person who was deemed "schizophrenic" was unconsciously trying to save the faltering marriage of his or her parents. By becoming crazy the young person distracted the parents from their own conflicts and stimulated them to come together in an effort to rescue their son or daughter.

I think Haley overgeneralizes: not all cases fit this pattern. However, on one point I find him particularly persuasive: many psychiatrically labeled persons I have met *were* reacting in a socially troubling way to unacknowledged conflicts of other family members. The tragedy of traditional therapy, Haley argues, is that by confirming the young person as mentally sick, he or she becomes the scapegoat for other family members—who are thus defined as having no serious problems—and is trapped into a lifetime career as a professional mental patient.[10]

Unfortunately, neither the work of Laing or Szasz nor that of Minuchin or Haley had much effect on the mental health system as a whole. Laing's work with schizophrenics, based on the idea that schizophrenia was in essence a spiritual crisis rather than a disease, spawned a few therapeutic asylums for "schizophrenics," such as the highly successful Soteria House (designed by psychiatrists Loren Mosher and Alma Menn). But these had disappeared by the mid-1970s after the countercultural ferment of the 1960s had dissipated.[11]

Szasz's writings also motivated a number of vigorous civil rights-minded lawyers to establish legal precedents in the 1960s that restricted the power of psychiatrists to impose unwanted "treatments" on the "mentally ill." In a variety of ways psychiatrists proved successful in circumventing these legal restrictions in the 1970s, 1980s and 1990s.

As family therapists became integrated into the psychiatric-industrial complex that was receiving a massive infusion of funds from the pharmaceutical companies, they abandoned the idea that "crazy" behavior was a response to interpersonal conflicts in the family and redefined the meaning of "family therapy" as practiced with "schizophrenics." For most therapists family therapy no longer means, as it does for Haley and Minuchin, exploring and modifying interpersonal dynamics that cause one or more family members to become "psychotic."[12] It is now understood as merely seeing the family as a whole in the treatment setting.

Most family therapists have now adopted the process that Haley had critiqued (see above) and no longer attempt to prevent "the identified patient" from being labeled and confirmed as mentally ill. As "family therapists" they now work as junior allies of the psychiatric establishment, helping to convince the "healthy" family members to accept and cope with the ostensibly tragic and inexorable fact that one of their members is chronically mentally ill and needs to be on powerful psychotropic drugs for the rest of his or her life.

The specter of the widespread development of nonmedical alternatives to the treatments for the problems of life that appeared in the 1960s had been exorcised by 1990, and the dominance of psychiatry within the mental health system was securely established once again.

The Woodstock of Psychotherapy

Yet in 1985 there were still pockets of therapists dispersed throughout the country who believed that the therapy profession was on the eve of a revolution, a transition to a more humanistic, less traditional, less pharmaceutically oriented model. Approximately seven thousand of these therapists (including me) converged on Phoenix, Arizona, in 1985 for a conference sponsored by the Milton H. Erickson Foundation.[13] Virtually all of the major innovators in the profession were gathered there—mostly, but not exclusively, those who had rejected the idea of mental illness and who advocated for reforms in the mental health system—including R. D. Laing, Thomas Szasz, Salvador Minuchin and Jay Haley. The conference attendees, who were mostly under forty years old, were told on a number of occasions by the speakers that the future of therapy lay in their hands.

R. D. Laing was in good form. It had been arranged for Laing to interview a bona fide "paranoid schizophrenic"—whom he had never met before—in a private room, while an audience of several thousand therapists watched on a video screen in a conference hall downstairs. (Needless to say, the young woman was informed in advance of the arrangement.) Despite the fact that the woman, Christy, knew she was being watched, she readily opened up to Laing and shared with him the unusual ideas (e.g., there was a conspiracy out to "get her") that evidently had earned her the label of chronic psychotic. Laing did not attempt to talk her out of this idea (although he disagreed with her on occasion)—in fact, he agreed.

He stated, "I mean this whole setup is an enormous conspiracy, and you're right in the middle of the conspiracy just now." "So," he added with a chuckle, "if you came here to get away from the conspiracy, you haven't done very well." When she asked him what kind of conspiracy he was talking about, he said he thought it was a benign conspiracy, a sign that the "Universal Mind" (the term she had used earlier in the conversation) was "waking up." The conversation concluded with a lively discussion of some passages in the Bible.[14]

After her twenty-minute talk with Dr. Laing, she asked if she could accompany him downstairs to watch while he answered questions from the other therapists, a request that seemed to surprise even Laing himself. During the question period Laing responded caustically to one of the questioners who stated that nothing of value had occurred in Laing's interaction with Christy:

> This young lady sitting beside me is supposed to be an absolute paranoid schizophrenic on medication. [She had been withdrawn from medication at Laing's request a day or two before their dialogue.] She's sitting here just now perfectly *compos mentis,* perfectly clear, facing this most intimidating situation from the stage, not exhibiting any symptoms of schizophrenic disorder. If you knew of any medication that could do that in twenty minutes, from there to here, would you say you wouldn't give that to a patient? You would have to spend the rest of your life being a biochemist to understand what the chemical effects of that sort of thing is supposed to be in the central nervous system. So you don't know anything about this sort of process. Have the humility to admit that, and keep your place![15]

After a number of questions, some curious, some appreciative, some critical, the young woman asked to make a few remarks in conclusion. "I don't go around like a paranoid schizophrenic all the time. I know how to keep my cool, and I think this guy [Laing] would be a great psychotherapist, because he does that . . . because he knows how to tap into other people's minds . . . not by just asking questions and trying to figure things out like some doctors."[16]

At this point Salvador Minuchin emerged from the audience to express his own appreciation of Laing and Christy's interaction and to reprimand the audience for what he took to be their failure to grasp the implications of what had occurred.

> I think you should learn something from Ronald. Because I don't think you did. You see, what we have experienced here is a communion of love. What I was observing, and I felt entranced, I felt in love with this young person, and she was able to elicit from Ronald, and so did he from her—that kind of experience. It was experience at the level not of words, but there was an element of joining, that was expressed in their hands, in their legs, they were moving exactly in the same place, and I loved it. And I think it's important that you should know that. I am talking to the physician that talks about drugs. Because the drug that existed there is very, very powerful.[17]

Minuchin was underscoring the point that what had occurred between Laing and Christy challenged one of the primary dogmas we had all been taught to believe in graduate school: that "schizophrenics" are not capable of forming relationships, that they are not amenable to therapy and that the most therapists can do is to help them to function on a very low level by maintaining them on "medication." Yet Laing had managed to win Christy's trust in a very short period of time, and his acceptance of her enabled her to manifest her own intelligence and charm. Although Laing and Minuchin had different theoretical orientations, both of them were iconoclasts who were critical of the ways in which the dogmas of the mental health profession limited the individual's capacity to grow and to change. Both were critical of the profession's reliance upon psychiatric drugs.

Laing's dialogue with Christy was in stark contrast to a dialogue he reproduced in his book written in 1982, *The Voice of Experience*,[18] between one of the most highly regarded psychoanalysts in the century, Wilfred Bion, and his schizophrenic patient. Bion advocated that interpretations should be "simple," "exact" and "mature." What follows is an excerpt from Bion's session with his patient:

PATIENT: I picked a tiny piece of my skin from my face and feel quite
             empty.
ANALYST: The tiny piece of skin is your penis, which you have torn
             out, and all your insides have come with it.
PATIENT: I do not understand . . . penis . . . only syllables and now it
             has no meaning.
ANALYST: You have split my word "penis" into syllables and now it
             has no meaning.

In the next session the exchange went as follows:

PATIENT: I cannot find any interesting food. I do not feel able to buy
             any new clothes and my socks are a mass of holes.
ANALYST: By picking out the tiny piece of skin yesterday you injured
             yourself so badly you can not even buy clothes; you're
             empty and have nothing to buy them with.
PATIENT: Although they are full of holes, they constrict my foot.
ANALYST: Not only did you tear out your own penis, but also mine.
             So today there is no interesting food—only a hole, a sock.
             But even the sock is made of a mass of holes, all of which
             you made and which have joined together to constrict, or
             swallow and injure, your foot.[19]

Evidently this and subsequent sessions proved to Bion that the patient
was so delusional that he believed he had literally eaten Bion's penis,
leaving a persecuting hole the patient felt a need to fill up. Ten days later
Bion reported, "A tear came from his [the patient's] eye and he said with
a mixture of despair and reproach, 'Tears come from my ears now.' "[20]

Laing remarks wryly that it is no wonder tears were coming from his
ears after having to listen to Bion's absurd interpretations day after day,
week after week, month after month, year after year. (This psychoanalysis
went on for years, we are told, which is not unusual.) While Bion's statements
are entirely fantastic, the patient's statements seem to convey simply and
exactly (albeit metaphorically) that what Bion is saying makes absolutely no
sense to the patient. Laing remarks that "it is difficult to fathom the difference
between Bion's psychoanalytic fantasies and what is usually called a psychotic

delusional system."[21] It is in fact the analyst here, the "expert," who seems more "out of contact" with reality than the patient.

Although Laing says that the two individuals are "equally crazy," he goes on to make the point that the patient is in fact making a profound communication when he states that tears were coming from his ears. If Laing were seeing such a patient, he says he can imagine a sigh. "I might be caught by his talent to say so much in so little. . . . I could not help but feel that the tears in his ears might betoken a sense on his part, which I can not help but share, of something sad, maybe even pathetic, about our relationship. There is truly an abyss between these two men."[22]

If Laing had conversed with Bion's patient, one imagines that the patient would have felt understood, as Christy did. But Bion as a psychoanalyst was more interested in fitting the patient into the procrustean bed of his own theories than in communicating with him as a fellow human being. It is no wonder that psychoanalysts reach the conclusion that schizophrenics are unable to form relationships with therapists.[23]

Working as a Family Therapist

I returned to New York from the Phoenix conference inspired by the idea that as a therapist I would not only be helping clients but working to transform the field. I had personally witnessed many of the family therapy innovators transform individuals—even those considered "severely mentally ill" by psychiatrists—in brief (one- to six-month) periods of time. In 1987 I began studying family therapy with Jay Haley and working at a clinic in Clifton, New Jersey. I was impressed with the power of family therapy to effect dramatic changes in individuals in short periods of time. One client I had was a thirty-five-year-old woman, Kathy, who was a single mother estranged from her sixteen-year-old daughter, Kim. The daughter's hostility to her mother had become so intense that she had been living at a girlfriend's home for two weeks when Kathy came in for an appointment. The school was threatening to call the child welfare system and have the daughter placed in a foster-care home.

I soon discovered that Kim had been involved in typical adolescent conflict with her mother, conflict exacerbated by other family members. Every time the daughter, Kim, would have a fight with Kathy, she would go to her three uncles or to her grandmother for support. These were unwittingly undermining Kathy's ability to discipline her daughter and thus intensifying the conflict between them. As I recollected, these were typical adolescent disputes (e.g., what time Kim's curfew should be). But the relatives were siding with the daughter against the mother. I called the uncles on the telephone and they agreed to come in. They were all quite cooperative and readily accepted my interpretation that they were undermining Kathy's ability to exercise discipline over her daughter. I had the uncles come in for a second session, this time to meet with Kathy. All three pledged to her that they would support her decisions (unless a decision was highly unusual, which they did not expect).

The biggest difficulty was Kathy's mother, who was convinced that her daughter had "mental problems" and was thus not able to be a competent mother. She conveyed this message to Kim repeatedly, which made Kim very angry at her mother. The source of this mother's belief was the fact that some time before Kathy consulted me she had been seeing a therapist individually who told her she had a "personality disorder." Somehow Kathy's mother learned about this. I met with Kathy's mother twice alone and several times with Kathy.

I was surprised at how quickly I was able to disabuse the mother of the thought that her daughter was mentally disabled. I noted that the fact Kathy was holding two jobs and supporting three children without any kind of help from a man (the father's whereabouts were unknown, and he did not pay child support) was evidence of *superior* competence. Kathy's mother accepted my authority, and I restored her confidence in her daughter. She was also able to see how her own communications with Kim had undermined Kathy's ability to exercise parental discipline. In this case as in many others, I saw how traditional individual therapy, by focusing on individuals' putative deficiencies, created problems that did not exist or compounded already-existing problems. Within three weeks Kim moved back with her mother, and they began to develop a much more positive relationship. Only on two or three occasions during the year I worked at the clinic were they unable to negotiate conflicts without my help.

While I was working at the clinic, I discovered the writings of Peter Breggin, who confirmed my own sense that psychiatric drugs had a detrimental effect (for the most part) on clients. After reading his book

Psychiatric Drugs: Hazards to the Brain[24] I began to encourage my clients
who were on neuroleptic drugs (e.g., Haldol, Mellaril, Prolixin, Thorazine)
to gradually wean themselves off these drugs. Although my clients on
antipsychotic drugs did not like them and appreciated my confidence in
their ability to function without them, the psychiatrist in the clinic was
infuriated. Soon after that the director of the clinic regretfully explained
that he would have to ask me to resign. I continued to see clients privately
in my office in New York. In 1988 I met some of the leaders of what was
then known as the "mental patients liberation movement." At the sugges-
tion of George Ebert, the director of the Mental Patients Liberation
Alliance, I founded the Network Against Coercive Psychiatry to inform
people about psychiatric abuse in the United States.

I appeared on a number of television shows, including *Geraldo,* William F.
Buckley Jr.'s *Firing Line* and *The Oprah Winfrey Show* to expose and protest
the treatments of individuals in psychiatric wards around the country. I
also interviewed in-depth seven individuals who had "psychotic" breakdowns (five or more years before I had interviewed them) and who had
extricated themselves from the mental health system and gone on to lead
"normal" lives. None of them had been rehospitalized, and none of them
had taken any psychiatric drugs for at least five years. (At the time of this
publication it has been at least twelve years for each of these individuals.)

I integrated their material into a book I wrote as an indictment of the
mental health system and as a message of hope for all those who had been
told they were "chronically mentally ill" by mental health professionals.
The book is titled *Madness, Heresy and the Rumor of Angels: The Revolt
Against the Mental Health System,*[25] and it contained a foreword by Thomas
Szasz. Taking my cue from Laing I replaced the medical model with a
growth model and substituted the "root metaphor"[26] of spiritual crisis for
that of "mental illness."[27] (What are abnormal symptoms of illness in the
disease model are regarded by the growth model as normal crises integral
to the process of development.)

Drawing on postmodern philosophy and romantic literary criticism, I
realized that the narrative genre that enabled me to configure my subjects'
experience in the most coherent and meaningful fashion was that of *the
romance.*[28] The growth model conforms to the narrative genre of the

romance, since the latter often involves the conquest of obstacles through which the protagonist "grows" in spiritual maturity. In fact, the particular species of the romantic genre dealing with the maturation of youth termed *bildungsroman* was quite popular in modern European literature and had its roots ultimately in traditional folklore.

Thus for each subject I interviewed the events of his or her life, including the psychotic episodes and involvement with mental health system, emerged as a story of a quest, of an existential or an identity crisis, of a descent into madness, of spiritual visions, of a battle for survival and spiritual well-being against mental health professionals, and finally of triumph, of self-discovery, of spiritual growth (all typical phases of the romance).

My subjects' battle against the mental health profession had often been arduous. The narrative embraced by mental health experts depicts all patients as victims of an insidious process of mental illness or brain disease from which they will never be able to fully recover. This story was told by the authorities to my subjects and their relatives over and again and was presented as "scientific truth." Thus it is not surprising that there were long periods of time in which many of my subjects succumbed to the mental health professionals' conviction that they were chronically mentally ill. Yet they rebounded, resisted being stripped of their human dignity, fought to salvage their sense of self-respect as human beings and to assert their right to define themselves as creative beings rather than as chronic mental patients.

One woman in her late twenties had allowed mental health professionals to discourage her for ten years from returning to work or school or withdrawing from the psychiatric drugs that kept her in a stuporous state. She told me of her decision to stop taking Lithium: "It's strange that I waited that long—until the stakes were at the highest, when my body was used to years of psychiatric drugs. . . . It would have been easier if I had made the decision before ten years of psychiatric history, stigma and drugs. . . . It's like a concentration camp inmate fleeing—when it got so bad that it would have been better to have been shot in a field than live on like that. You know you have to break free, affirm your spirit, and try." Looking back five years later she described it as a spiritual experience of joy and pride, "a real sense of coming home and feeling myself for the first time in many years. I had finally claimed myself again in the fertile ground of my being."[29] All of the subjects in my book emerged from their crises months or years later with a stronger sense of self and direction, and with the determination never to take psychiatric medication again.

The same events are typically configured by mental health professionals into a tragic narrative about the gradual and insidious destruction, or at least the crippling, of the individual by "mental illness." The credibility of the mental health narrative requires that the patient conform to the definition of a victim of "schizophrenia," which according to the psychiatric profession is a chronic and incurable disease. Thus in order for this narrative account to retain its plausibility, the psychiatrist must—and does—engage in actions that are likely to discourage patients from undertaking those kinds of activities that would transform them from "abnormal" patients into "normal" persons (e.g., working at less-than-menial jobs). Thus the psychiatric narrative is a self-fulfilling prophecy.

I want to add here that in the nine years after going on television and radio and writing the book, I was contacted by over ten thousand victims or survivors of the mental health system. Although the vast majority of them called for help or advice, I spoke at some length to at least several hundred former patients who had had breakdowns and whose experience conformed to that of the subjects of my book: they extricated themselves from the mental health profession; they went back to work or school; they formed relationships; and they weaned themselves off psychiatric drugs.

Although I believe that the idea of mental illness has no therapeutic or explanatory value, I would not claim that *all* instances of madness can be subsumed under a growth-crisis model. There are probably a small number of individuals among the class deemed chronically mentally ill by psychiatrists who even with adequate emotional support and encouragement would be unable to adapt to their life situations or to the world *as it is today* without experiencing periodic "breakdowns." Yet I would not describe these individuals as "ill," merely as very sensitive. There is another group of individuals who are genuinely under any and all circumstances *mad*.[30] There is nothing *wrong* with these individuals—many of them are able to function quite well—although they could not adjust to the 9-to-5 work world. Nevertheless they are often highly creative, fascinating persons who have the potential to make contributions to the community from which they are invariably excluded by the practices of psychiatry.[31]

Those individuals who are psychotic and criminally inclined constitute a small minority of mental patients. I regard them as primarily criminals (and thus they fall outside the purview of this book); they are probably no more or less intractable than other criminals. (Although I believe that they should be subject to the same judicial penalties as "normal" criminals, I am not sanctioning the prison system as it exists today.)

Contrary to psychiatric propaganda, the interpretation of madness as mental illness or as a brain disease is not a scientific triumph but a value-laden enterprise that seeks to silence, suppress and demean mad people in the name of "curing" them. The problems of life that trouble persons who become defined as mental patients are not medical in nature (unless they are actual physical illnesses), and thus it is not surprising that "medical solutions" do not solve their problems. The main reason for the medical designation is to bring them under the hegemony of psychiatrists. This leads to identifying any communication on their part as a symptom of their illnesses—it thus precludes any kind of meaningful communication. As Michel Foucault wrote, "The constitution of madness as a mental illness, at the end of the eighteenth century, affords the evidence of a broken dialogue. . . . In the serene world of mental illness, modern man no longer communicates with the madman."[32] The psychiatric dogma is that schizophrenics are *unable* to form relationships. But as Laing pointed out long ago, it is more accurate to say that psychiatrists *refuse* to form relationships with schizophrenics. (Sometimes forming such a relationship involves the willingness to communicate in an unconventional manner.)

I have not had difficulty forming friendships with mad people. In 1991 I met a young mad woman named Lily when I was visiting a client in a halfway house. At first I did not realize how mad she was, since she appeared to be "normal." She was very attractive, well groomed, stylishly but casually dressed, and spoke in a quiet but self-assured manner. After I spent one afternoon talking to her, I realized that she was not only utterly mad but that she was also a genius in her own right.

Recently, postmodern philosophers such as Richard Rorty have argued that what philosophers have claimed to be "knowledge about objective reality" is really only conformity to culturally sanctioned norms of justification. Rorty makes a case that philosophy ought to be more concerned with "aesthetic enhancement" than with "getting things right." He argues that philosophy's consuming quest for "objective truth" (which he holds is a myth) has led to a restriction of the power of the imagination and a failure to accept and respect culturally deviant forms of perception and discourse. These "deviant forms" have the power to impart a poetic dimension to life and to "take us out of our old selves by the power of strangeness" and "aid us in becoming new beings."[33]

One need not completely endorse Rorty's skepticism to agree that we have drawn too firm a boundary between life and art, and that many mad people can help to make this boundary more fluid and thus contribute to aesthetically enhancing the "conversation of humanity" (to use Rorty's phrase). But this will not happen as long as we allow psychiatrists to continue to denigrate as a symptom of mental illness any statement that does not conform to what we conventionally take to be literal truth. For example, Lily inhabits a world far more enchanting than the one in which most people abide. She was not completely oblivious to "the real world." She told me quite believably that she grew up in the Bronx and went to parochial school until she was eighteen, when she had her first breakdown and was placed in a psychiatric hospital. I did not literally believe, however, her account of her birth: she said that she had been born prematurely in the Cyprus desert when her mother's covered wagon was knocked over en route from Cyprus to Jerusalem. When I followed her lead and tried to speak in her language, I found myself becoming increasingly poetic.

One time I asked her about a counselor that she had had a meeting with. "What was he like?" I asked. "Entenmann's cake," she responded. She said nothing more as if her meaning was self-evident. (She always did that, much to my amusement.) After a pause I said, "What do you mean 'Entenmann's cake'?" "Meaning sometimes he's fresh and resourceful like a cup of coffee that wakes you up in the morning, but other times he's stale and dry and has to have his own way."

One time she pointed to a bird outside her window which she said was a crow. She said that she gave it some bread crumbs to eat. I asked her if the crow ate the bread crumbs. She said no; it said to her, "There's lots and lots of worms to eat in the ground that's soaking wet. We appreciate your patronage of bread that's moist and well kept, and we will come to retrieve it when our thirst is quenched and wet." She stopped then as if she had uttered something as commonplace as "It's a nice day out today." "The crow said that to you?" I responded. Then she laughed and said with surprise, "Who do you think I am? Dr. Doolittle—a professor lost in time who knows how to talk to a bird with a rhythm and a rhyme?"

She was never at a loss for words and always had a fascinating story to tell. It was as if she dreamt it and then perceived it as real. (She is sufficiently aware of "the real world" that she is able to handle the challenges of traveling about in New York City.)

Of course the psychiatrists and social workers she came into contact with (with one or two exceptions among the social workers) had no appreciation for her artistry. They merely regarded her as an incurable case of schizophrenia and relegated her to the bottom of the social hierarchy. They invited her to go to day treatment programs where the "mentally ill" were sequestered, drugged ("medicated") and occupied with tasks like stuffing envelopes. She had enough self-respect to stay away.

For Lily there was no distinction between life and art. She was a poet and a court jester. Like the Marx brothers or André Breton or Salvador Dali, she did not perceive and describe the world "realistically"—she re-presented it in continually surprising and fascinating ways. I am thankful that the psychiatrists have not been able to "cure" her.

My Final Disillusionment

I had started out in psychiatry critical of the treatment of the "mentally ill." The more I experienced and read, the more critical I became of the mental health profession. My experience talking with thousands of individuals led me to believe that the mental health system is destructive—not just to mental patients but to hundreds of thousands of individuals in this country. I do not deny, of course, that some individuals have been helped to overcome the problems of life through the assistance of a benevolent therapist or even through a drug that raises their threshold for frustration or reduces their anxiety. But I am still adamantly opposed to the administration of neuroleptic drugs—drugs such as Thorazine, Stelazine, Prolixin, Haldol, Mellaril (more will be said about this later) and Lithium. I believe minor tranquilizers can sometimes be helpful (although long-term use of these drugs is probably unwise). The fact that certain drugs have calming effects upon people does not prove that the causes of their problems are biochemical in nature. There is always a correlation between psychological states and biochemical states—however, contrary to psychiatric convention, correlation does not entail causation. (This will be discussed later.)

The more friends and acquaintances I made among the victims of psychiatry, the more I became alienated from the mental health system and wanted to get out of the field of psychology altogether. At the same time, I felt more attracted to the church as the body of Christ and wanted to direct my efforts to "building it up" as an alternative to the mental health system. In order to do this I needed to undermine the dubious credibility of the mental health profession and work within the church to resist and change the status quo. If I am going to help people with their "problems" in the future, I want to do it as a servant of Christ, not as a "mental health professional."

2

Psychiatry's Invasion of Family & Community Life

I
n 1994 journalist Joe Sharkey, who had previously been an assistant
national editor for the *Wall Street Journal*, wrote a book titled *Bedlam:
Greed, Profiteering and Fraud in a Mental Health System Gone Crazy.*[1]
This is the story of the astronomical growth of investor-owned psychiatric
hospitals during the 1980s, which Sharkey aptly refers to as "the Recovery
Era." In this period broader insurance coverage was available for an
ever-growing range of disorders, addictions and behavioral problems. The
methods employed by hospitals to recruit patients were unscrupulous
(including in some cases actual kidnapping). Representative Patricia
Schroeder, chairwoman of the U.S. House of Representatives Select
Committee on Children, Youth and Families, described this development
as "one of the most disgraceful and scandalous episodes in the history of
health care in America."[2]

In 1984 there were 220 for-profit psychiatric hospitals in the United
States. Four years later there were 440.[3] Although these hospitals are
privately owned, they subsist at the public trough. Some of their
revenue comes directly from the federal government, which began
providing medical insurance in 1965, and some comes from private
insurers, whose behavior is channeled by subsidies, tax preferences and
state-level regulation. By 1990 twenty-nine states would mandate that
employers provide in-patient coverage for mental health care; forty-

one, coverage for alcoholism; and twenty-seven, coverage for drug abuse. Sharkey wrote,

> By the end of the '80s, millions of Americans who had never before come into contact with psychiatry were using greatly-expanded health insurance benefits and spending stretches of time in the new psychiatric hospitals, twenty to thirty days on average, rather than the five or six days a patient with a serious medical problem might spend in the general hospital. It was a triumph of medically-oriented psychiatry, a profession which, according to psychiatrist Peter Breggin, exists now at "the political center of a multi-billion-dollar psycho-pharmaceutical complex that pushes biological and genetic theories as well as drugs on the society. It is a political institution licensed by the State, financed by government, and empowered by the courts."[4]

A disproportionately large share of the victims of this expansion were children and adolescents. In 1989 services rendered to them accounted for well over one billion of the three billion dollars paid to private psychiatric hospitals for in-patient treatments. Children were attractive to this industry because they stayed in the hospital far longer and were charged more money, due to the policies of insurance companies.[5]

A marketing executive told the trade publication *Advertising Age* in the 1980s, "There's a new market out there in grammar and high school aged kids."[6] In 1987 the American Medical Association's official newspaper, *American Medical News,* reported that "psychiatric admissions to private hospitals nearly tripled between 1980 and 1986 for those younger than eighteen. . . . The hospitalization rates have been particularly startling given that the population of ten- to nineteen-year-olds declined 11% from 1980 to 1987."[7]

Writing in 1994, Sharkey estimated that well over 300,000 adolescents and children each year are placed in psychiatric hospitals and treatment centers, both private and public, and that the numbers are still growing. A recent industry survey indicated that between 1989 and 1990 the number of admissions of children under thirteen increased by nearly 25 percent.[8]

How does one explain this rapid increase in the number of children hospitalized? In the spring of 1992 Representative Schroeder quoted from a Justice Department briefing:

> Current intelligence shows psychiatric hospitals and clinics are defrauding government programs and private insurers of hundreds of millions of dollars annually. . . . Our investigative team found that thousands of adolescents, children and adults have been hospitalized for a psychiatric care they really did not need. . . . Documents, affidavits, and testimony obtained by the Committee will show a systematic plan to bilk patients of their hard-earned dollars, strip them of their dignity, and leave them worse off than before they went for help.[9]

A 1990 federal review of five hundred psychiatric in-patient cases found that two-thirds of them did not need to be hospitalized.[10] A 1993 study by the New York State Commission on Quality Care for the Mentally Disabled found that more than half of the children in state-run psychiatric residences did not belong there and that "three-quarters of the children had no psychotic symptoms and almost all were receiving psychotropic drugs."[11] Jim Kent, vice-president of the National Health Professional Programs Corporation Managed Care Company in Tampa, estimated that 80 percent of adolescent admissions were unnecessary.[12]

Most of the new patients were actually taken to the hospital by their parents. The parents were responding to a marketing campaign designed to exploit their insecurities. Television and newspaper ads defined everything from poor grades to coming home late for dinner as symptoms of mental illness. They exhorted anxious parents to take their children in for psychiatric exams before it was too late. Professor Ira Schwartz of the University of Michigan described the ads as "very seductive and misleading." He stated,

> They essentially tell parents this message: if your child is having difficulty then you owe it to yourself, as a responsible parent, to bring your child into a hospital for diagnostic assessment. If you don't, the ads usually say, something very terrible can happen to your child. They could end up in jail or committing suicide. In addition, of course, the ads remind parents that their insurance will pick up the tab.[13]

The ads invariably cautioned parents that many childhood or adolescent problems would not respond to out-patient or brief in-patient treatment.

The programs that the hospitals offered were, for the most part, uniformly punitive and repressive. They seemed designed to turn children into docile conformists, to make them submit to arbitrary rules, to suppress individual initiative. Often the methods used seemed similar to those one would find employed in prisoner-of-war camps. Schwartz described these programs in the *Journal of Adolescent Health Care* in 1989.

> They typically consist of rigid and punitive behavior modification regimes . . . characterized by excessive and lengthy use of isolation and solitary confinement, often for minor misbehavior and rule infractions; mail censorship; and restricted or absolute prohibitions on visitation and use of a telephone. Even more disturbing is the fact that there is evidence that the administrative and medical staff in some hospitals refuse to correct abuse documented by official authorities and only do so when threatened with legal action.[14]

In a discussion in 1992 Schwartz told Sharkey that on visits to more than one hundred hospitals with psychiatric units for children, he personally encountered instances of "rage reduction therapy—programs characterized by excessive use of restraint, handcuffs, solitary confinement," not to mention "very primitive behavior-modification regimes where kids start out in some cases wearing pajamas and have to earn points so that they can wear their own clothes, or even earn points to get better fed."[15]

The effects of hospitalization may continue long afterward. Many of the children come to believe that they are in effect "mentally ill." All of them are labeled with a diagnosis that persists on their medical records and that may create future problems in employment or in obtaining health insurance coverage. Curtis Decker, an advocate for patients' rights, states, "We have reports of many children refusing to return home because they feel betrayed by their parents, even though the parents may have had good intentions. . . . So not only does the child receive a great deal of damage in the course of their treatment, but it lives long after their experience in the psychiatric facility."[16]

In January 1994 an episode of the *Oprah Winfrey Show* was devoted to a debate on the phenomenon of placing children and adolescents in psychiatric hospitals. As a participant in this debate[17] I had the opportunity to meet a bright seventeen-year-old named Naomi Clements who was dedicated to making the public aware of the abusiveness of psychiatric hospitals. Her parents had been worried because she smoked marijuana when she was fourteen and spent time with youths several years older than her—although she continued to maintain her grades and keep up with her schoolwork. Persuaded by slick advertisements that Naomi's spirit of adolescent independence—or rebelliousness—came from a mental disorder, they hospitalized her against her will. In the hospital she was placed on Lithium and told that she was chronically "manic-depressive" and that just as a diabetic needed to take insulin, Naomi would need to take Lithium for the rest of her life. (Lithium is a highly toxic drug. It can cause damage to the heart, kidneys and liver.) Naomi's reluctance to conform to the draconian rules of the hospitals that housed her was interpreted as pathological resistance. On one occasion she was put in isolation and strapped to a bed for three days. Another time she was placed in seclusion for thirteen days; at this point she made a desperate attempt to get out by eating the room's only light bulb. (The ploy was successful: she was rushed to a regular hospital for treatment.)

Although Naomi recovered from the physical ordeal, the emotional wounds remained. Her parents told Oprah Winfrey that they regretted institutionalizing her and believed that they had been duped by psychiatry. Nevertheless their relationship with their daughter was still strained.

What must be emphasized here is the complicity of mental health professionals in what psychiatrist Peter Breggin aptly termed "the war against children." This is often ignored by the media and hence by the public. While hospitals have been justifiably attacked as blindly pursuing private profits, it is usually implied—if only by omission of any discussion of their role—that mental health professionals adhere to a higher code of ethics. The law stipulates that in order for hospitalization to occur, it must first be authorized by a mental health professional after doing a "psychological evaluation"; thus had professionals refused to authorize the hospitalizations that were unnecessary (according to the government studies described above, page 38) they would not have occurred. Furthermore the hospitals would not have been able to bill insurance companies or the government for the cost of hospitalization if mental health professionals had not filled out forms declaring that the patients were ill enough to require hospitalization.

There is another more subtle form of complicity: Mental health professionals create a climate of thought and opinion that seems to make hospitalization for normal teenagers a viable option. They have systematically been attempting to medicalize all the problems of life for the past few decades. When government researchers determined that most of the children and adolescents who were hospitalized did not belong there, they were employing common sense. But mental health standards are at odds with common sense, since many normal behaviors are now viewed by them as symptoms of mental illness requiring psychiatric treatment. For instance, one of the most common diagnoses used to justify incarcerating children in mental hospitals is oppositional defiant disorder as described by the *Diagnostic and Statistical Manual of Mental Disorders*. (The DSM III R was the edition used in the late 1980s.[18]) According to the DSM III R, children with oppositional defiant disorder "commonly are argumentative with adults, frequently lose their tempers, swear and are often angry, resentful and easily annoyed by others. They frequently actively defy adult requests and rules and deliberately annoy other people. They tend to blame others for their own mistakes or difficulties." I think most persons would realize that this description fits the normal child—perhaps on a bad day. As Breggin observed, "It encompasses every kid in the world who's got any gumption."[19]

Finally, the inhumane nature of the programs designed by mental health professionals to restore the "mental health" of youth is a tragic commentary on their callous indifference to children's welfare and their readiness to subordinate humanitarian and moral concerns to the objective of creating an efficient and financially lucrative business.

The Learning Disabilities Scam
The reader may not be surprised that investors in private hospitals were willing to enrich themselves financially at the expense of the welfare of

children. After all, business executives do not have a reputation of being protectors of the public. But mental health professionals have presented themselves (for the most part successfully, with the assistance of a well-financed public relations campaign) as protectors and promoters of America's mental health. Undoubtedly their status has been bolstered by the reputation that medical doctors in general hold in the public mind as virtually omniscient initiates of the sacrosanct discipline of medical science, possessing a saintlike devotion to the well-being of their patients and an unwavering dedication to the advancement of scientific knowledge.

The 1970s and 1980s saw the growth of a new industry whose very existence depends upon the trust and the respect the public holds for the mental health professions—the learning disabilities industry. The market once again was children, and the method of expansion was to convince parents that their normal children suffered from a disability that would prevent them from learning unless they were administered powerful psychiatric drugs (for the most part Ritalin—an amphetamine or, more colloquially, "speed"), and placed in special classrooms where they are taught by special-education experts and monitored by school psychologists and psychiatrists.

Before 1965 virtually no children (except for the developmentally disabled) were deemed to have a learning disability. But after the disease was "invented," the phenomenon took off. As Gerald Coles, associate professor of clinical psychiatry at Rutgers Medical School, observed:

> Learning disability rose meteorically in the schools and the professions, and its partisans presented it as a field that had already had its own history, experts and special techniques . . . . By the end of the decade, children began to be classified as learning disabled, Federal funds were appropriated for LD curricula, an array of tests and remedial materials were devised and published, parents' groups were organized, LD graduate-school programs were opened, the number of journal articles and books on the subject multiplied, a profusion of LD research projects commenced, and pharmaceutical companies promoted and profited from drugs for the learning disabled—in all, learning disabilities suddenly became a growth industry.[20]

From 1976 to 1983 the number of children classified as learning

disabled in schools went from approximately 800,000 to 1.8 million.[21]
Today the most common form of learning disability is termed "Attention
Deficit/Hyperactivity Disorder" (ADHD), as it is listed in the *Diagnostic
and Statistical Manual of Mental Disorders*. It was estimated in 1994 that
over 3.5 million children in the United States were diagnosed as having
ADHD.[22]

Towson State University professor Richard Vatz wrote in the *Wall Street
Journal*, "[The diagnosis] relieves children, their parents and teachers of
responsibility for misbehavior and incompetence where those are precisely
the problems; it justifies claims for special treatment in school and at work;
and it provides financial rewards and status for a large population of the
mental health and pharmaceutical fields."[23]

Dr. Fred Baughman, a pediatric neurologist, wrote in a letter to the *New
York Times*, "The invention of diseases satisfied medical-economic needs.
Additional income for a growing number of psychologists and psychiatrists is generated. . . . Presently child psychiatrists, psychologists, counselors and special educators in and around in the U.S. public schools nearly
outnumber teachers."[24]

Diane McGuinness undertook an exhaustive survey of the literature in
the field.[25] Judging from data in 1985, McGuinness estimated that 10 to
15 percent of the total school population were officially classified as
ADHD. On the basis of two surveys, however, she believes that teachers
informally "treat approximately one-third of all elementary-school boys as
an abnormal population because they are fidgety, inattentive, and unamen-
able to adult control."[26]

She presents compelling evidence that this so-called disease does not
exist. "The past twenty-five years has led to a phenomenon almost unique
in medical history. Methodologically rigorous research indicates that Attention Deficit Disorder and hyperactivity as 'syndromes' simply do not
exist. We have invented a disease, given it medical sanction, and now must
disown it."[27] Yet she concludes rather ruefully, "There is now so much
machinery in motion to promote a diagnosis of deviance for perfectly
normal behavior that it seems almost impossible to slow it down, much
less bring it to a halt."[28]

Before describing the studies disproving the existence of ADHD, I want to call the reader's attention to enlightening statements made by a few advocates of common sense. Peter Schrag and Diane Divoky wrote:

> As a consequence [of psychiatric labeling], millions of children are no longer regarded as part of the ordinary spectrum of human personality and intelligence—children who are quieter or brighter than the average, children who are jumpy, children who are slow—but as people who are qualitatively different from the "normal" population, individuals who, as a consequence of "minimal brain dysfunction," "hyperactivity" or "functional behavior disorders" constitute a distinct and separate group. . . . These are not sick children or people with obvious physical or psychological handicaps: they are healthy children—poor, affluent, bright, slow, black, white—who come from an ordinary spectrum of homes, live in ordinary towns and go to ordinary schools.[29]

The well-known educator John Holt said, "Given the fact that some children are more energetic and active than others, might it not be easier, more healthy, and more humane to deal with this fact by giving them more time and scope to make use of and work off their energy? . . . Everyone is taken care of, except, of course, the child himself, who wears a label which to him reads clearly enough 'freak' and who is denied from those closest to him, however much sympathy he may get, what he and all children most need—respect, faith, hope and trust."[30]

Numerous studies have shown that on a variety of experimental tasks, children labeled as having "attention deficit disorders" perform comparably to the control group of "normal" subjects. McGuinness documents that studies measuring sustained attention to a problem-solving task between ADD children and their controls have shown no difference, "indicating that not only are they not deficient in attentional control but are equal to other children in highly complex cognitive problem-solving skills." She concludes, "These studies, carried out in laboratory settings, away from the classroom that the child appears to find problematic, and providing the necessary control over IQ, reading level, and so forth, show that when ADD children are matched for initial ability with the control group, their performance is essentially identical. What differences do appear seem to reflect their unwillingness to persist in tasks that they do not prefer."[31] In studies where they are required to perform routinized, boring, repetitive tasks, these children are less motivated and thus perform less well than the control group—unless they are given extrinsic rewards for their performance.

The studies reveal that the ADD children in fact do not suffer from cognitive deficits but are simply less motivated to perform some of the kinds of tasks required in school. Their poor academic performance is thus not a result of disability but of a lack of motivation. This would indicate that by categorizing these children as defective, professionals are scapegoating them for the failure of teachers to engage their attention. This is why John Gatto, who taught school in New York City for twenty-six years, stated that it is the children with the most resistance to the regimentation, systemization, standardization and conformity prevalent in the school system who are most likely to be labeled. "Those children with most natural genius . . . the fittest to be human have the least resistance to inhumanity."[32]

Gatto blames the practices of the schools—not the children—for poor academic performance. He wrote,

David learns to read at age four; Rachel, at age nine: in normal development when both are thirteen you can't tell which one learned first—the five-year spread means nothing at all. But in school I will label Rachel "learning disabled" and slow David down a bit, too. . . . In twenty years of teaching rich kids and poor I almost never met a "learning disabled" child; hardly ever met a "gifted and talented" one either. Like all school categories, these are sacred myths, created by the human imagination. . . .

I taught public school for twenty-six years, but I just can't do it anymore. . . . I can't train children to wait to be told what to do; I can't train people to drop what they're doing when a bell sounds; I can't persuade children to feel some justice in their [social] class position when there isn't any.[33]

As I noted earlier, mental health professionals and special educators promote Ritalin (the generic name is methlyphenidate) as the cure for ADD. In October 1995 there were two million children and teenagers on Ritalin—four times as many as in 1990.[34]

In McGuinness's extensive review of the literature she finds no evidence that medication had any positive effect whatsoever on school performance. "The children on a drug regime continued to show evidence of poor academic skills and poor social adjustment, despite taking drugs."[35] Although children do not like the drugs and most plead to be taken off after the first year, they are generally kept on the drugs for at least five years. McGuinness notes that numerous follow-up studies "indicate that children on a long drug-treatment program feel worthless and have extremely low self-esteem."[36]

Most parents are duped into putting their children on Ritalin. As Breggin notes, they are not told that years of research and clinical use have failed to confirm any positive long-term effects from Ritalin on behavior or academic performance. Even the National Institute of Mental Health admits that although the drugs improve "compliance and sustained attention," they seem "less reliable in bringing about associated improvements, at least of an enduring nature, in social-emotional and academic problems."[37]

Parents are not told that Ritalin can cause the very things it is supposed to cure—inattention, hyperactivity and aggression. When this happens the child is likely to be given higher doses of the drug (or an even stronger agent), resulting in a vicious circle of increasing drug toxicity.[38] Nor are parents informed that Ritalin can cause permanent disfiguring tics and that it can suppress growth. Perhaps most importantly, as Breggin notes, "Finally, parents will not be told by their doctor that *there are almost guaranteed non-drug methods of improving the conduct of nearly all so-called DBD [Destructive Behavior Disorders] children—through more interesting, engaging schools and through more rationally managed, loving family relationships*" (emphasis added).[39]

The Electroshock Lobby

Perhaps the most potent symbol of the powerlessness of the humanistic movement within the mental health system today is the resurgence of electroshock treatment, which is also known as electroconvulsive therapy (ECT). Electroschock treatment had become virtually extinct in the 1970s, but today it is given annually to at least 100,000 persons.[40]

It is beyond the scope of this book to document in detail the deceptive manner in which a skillful marketing strategy has been utilized by the psychiatric profession to sell ECT, justify its rebirth and overcome the negative image that it had acquired among the American population, due in large part to the movie *One Flew Over the Cuckoo's Nest* as well as other adverse publicity.[41] The key to this advertising campaign is to foster the misconception that the "old" ECT was destructive while the "new" ECT is essentially a miracle cure with no adverse side effects.[42]

Both the research conducted on ECT and the public marketing of ECT (based on the research) by the psychiatric profession is completely untrustworthy. The most vigorous promoters of and public lobbiers for ECT are a few psychiatrists who have done much of the current "research" on ECT. In addition, they have written most of the reviews of the research on ECT. These psychiatrists not only use ECT regularly but also serve as paid consultants to ECT machine-manufacturing companies, from which they derive considerable additional income, including royalties for promotional videotapes. The most prominent ECT expert in the United States, Richard Abrams, actually co-owns an ECT company, Somatics, Inc., which manufacturers at least one-half of the ECT machines sold worldwide, and which Abrams acknowledged in a deposition in 1991 is the source of 50 percent of his income.[43] It is the psychiatrists who use ECT who have shaped the American Psychiatric Association's (APA) official policy on ECT.

The American Psychiatric Association's 1990 Task Force Report on ECT cited nine of Abrams's publications in the general bibliography, making him by far the most represented author.[44] It placed his 1989 textbook on its recommended reading list for professionals, which contains approximately a dozen books—none by critics of ECT such as Breggin or neurologist John Friedberg, nor by any of the ECT patients who have written books and articles critical of ECT. It also recommends both for professionals and for the public a videotape originally made by electroshock promoter Dr. Max Fink for the company Abrams owns, as well as advertising handouts published by manufacturers of electroshock machines.

The American Psychiatric Association has concluded that ECT is safe and effective. What weight shall we give this conclusion when we consider that it is based primarily on research conducted by individuals who substantially profit from the use of ECT, including the owner of an electroshock machine-manufacturing company? It is common knowledge that researchers hired by cigarette companies denied for decades any causal link between cigarettes and lung cancer. The public has no reason to believe that scientists who derive substantial income from the use of ECT will be any more truthful about the risks of their product than researchers for cigarette companies were about tobacco. But surely it is reasonable to expect a professional organization composed of doctors, sworn to uphold the Hippocratic oath, to act with more commitment to the public weal than cigarette manufacturers! Why then has the American Psychiatric Association failed to establish an ethical standard for conducting psychiatric research—for example, that research on ECT must be done by scientists who do not make their living administering ECT or selling machines and other materials related to the use of ECT? Is it because the American Psychiatric Association, in violation of the public trust, places the financial interests of its members above the welfare of the American people? Melton Schwartz, a professor of psychiatry and co-owner of Somatics, Inc., revealingly stated, "Psychiatrists don't make much money and by practicing ECT they can bring their income up to the level of the family practitioner or internist."[45] (According to the American Medical Association, psychiatrists earned in 1995 an average of $132,000—which many Americans would hardly consider a substandard income.) Schwartz also said that his profits from Somatics are comparable to having an additional psychiatric practice.

This conflict of interest is troubling not merely because critics of ECT have presented evidence that it is no more effective than sham ECT (where patients actually received only an anesthetic) but also because they have made a persuasive argument that it produces permanent memory loss and brain damage.[46] For reasons of space, in this chapter I want to restrict the focus to ECT's particularly deleterious effects on the elderly, who are today the largest group of individuals receiving ECT.[47]

In the most extensive study on ECT-related deaths yet done (1957), psychiatrist David Impastato investigated 254 deaths: 214 from published accounts and 40 previously unpublished. Although a staunch supporter of ECT, Impastato acknowledged that it was a "risky" procedure, particularly for the elderly. Most of the fatalities had received unmodified ECT. He estimated an overall death rate of one per thousand and one per two hundred in persons over sixty years old. In 235 of the cases Impastato was able to determine the cause of death: there were one hundred "cardiovascular deaths" (43 percent), sixty-six "cerebral deaths" (about 28 percent), forty-three "respiratory deaths" (18 percent) and twenty-six deaths from other causes (11 percent).[48]

Although the ECT lobby claims that the new electroshock has reduced the mortality rates significantly, prominent supporters of ECT such as Impastato and Lothar Kalinowsky as well as critics such as Breggin believe that the recent ECT modifications have increased the mortality rate, as well as other hazards, by adding the complications of pharmacological muscle paralysis and anesthesia.[49]

A 1982 study also underlines the risk of ECT for elderly persons with heart problems. Of forty-two persons undergoing modified (the new) ECT during a one-year period (1975-1976) at the Payne Whitney Clinic in New York City, seventeen (40 percent) had presented with heart disease. Twelve of the seventeen (70 percent) developed heart complications. Eleven of the twelve were over age sixty. Nine of the twelve developed arrhythmias; four of the complications were life-threatening. Forty-five minutes after her fifth treatment one patient sustained a cardio-pulmonary arrest and died.[50]

A study done at Washington University in St. Louis and another study done at Cornell Medical Center in New York in the mid-1980s found ECT recipients suffered increased risk of heart and lung problems, as well as pneumonia.[51]

In 1993 David Kroessler and Barry Fogel compared the mortality rates of individuals over eighty years old given ECT as opposed to individuals over eighty given medication as treatments for depression.[52] After one year, over 25 percent of the ECT-treated group had died compared to 3.6 percent of the non-ECT patients. This recent study of sixty-five patients provides strong evidence that there was an *extremely* high death rate from ECT for very old patients.[53]

Friedberg stated that as increasing numbers of elderly patients are shocked, increasing numbers will die.[54] Michael Shavin, formerly chief of anesthesiology at Bay Coast Medical Center in Baytown, Texas, stopped doing shock treatments in 1993, reducing his income by $75,000 a year. Although it was difficult for Shavin to give up the income, his conscience would not allow him to continue. "I began to get very disturbed by what I was seeing," he said. "We had many elderly patients repeatedly getting shocks, ten or twelve in a series, getting more disoriented each time." Shavin believes that the cardiovascular system is dramatically stressed both by electroshock and anesthesia. He said, "As an anesthesiologist, what I do for three to five minutes can have serious consequences later. But psychiatrists cannot bring themselves to admit any harm from ECT unless the patient gets electrocuted to death on the table while being videotaped and observed by a United Nations task force. The deaths are telling us something; psychiatrists don't want to hear it."[55]

The American Psychiatric Association claims that candidates for electroshock (mostly elderly women) are afflicted with "clinical depression." The APA overlooks the various environmental factors that are probably at the root of their unhappiness: in many cases their husbands have died, many of their friends have died, they may not have children who live near them—they may have no support network. Breggin stated that if an elderly woman goes to the typical psychiatrist she will not get

> help in redeveloping her social life, she's not likely to get connected to a volunteer program. . . . She is not likely to get help to be reattached to her community in general. . . . The psychiatrist, by all odds a male, is not likely to reach into *his heart* to try to fill her empty heart. He has other ideas in mind: drugs and electro-shock treatment. . . . We actually don't have a disease. It's a feeling of hopelessness. We don't have a disease and we don't have a treatment. What psychiatrists do is to inflict a closed head injury on people in spiritual crises.[56]

Several years ago I was consulted by a thirty-five-year-old African-American woman, "Ruby," and her eighty-year-old grandmother, "Alice," who had raised her. The grandmother had had a series of electroshock treatments and was given antidepressants; neither of these "treatments" alleviated her depression. I questioned the two of them for an hour and was able to discover the source of the problem. Ruby was planning on moving several hours away to live with her fiancé, and it was her intention to leave Alice behind to save her the stress of moving. Alice knew about this and was unhappy but reluctant to say anything. It was obvious to me, considering that Alice had no family in New York, that she experienced Ruby's intended move as an abandonment. Alice dreaded being left alone. When I explained this to her, she acknowledged it to be true. I asked Ruby if she was willing to find a studio apartment for her grandmother close to where she and her fiancé would live. Without hesitation she agreed.

I spoke to Ruby one month later, just before she was planning to move, and she stated that her grandmother's depression had entirely cleared up. Thus in one hour without any further "therapeutic sessions," without drugs or electro-therapy, I was able to alleviate her "clinical depression." I do not believe that my intervention and solution required any kind of advanced training in psychology or, for that matter, any profound insight into human nature. Unfortunately, people have become so reliant on and mystified by mental health professionals that they frequently cannot see what is patently obvious.

The resurgence of ECT is yet another example of the mental health system's colonization of populations previously outside its control. Such colonization is the baneful effect of psychiatrists' influence and of their willingness to subordinate the welfare of human beings to the desire to boost their fortunes and increase their power.

The Colonization of the World's Population by the Mental Health System

The expansionist dynamic of the mental health system manifests itself in a relentless quest to transform people (almost entirely) into patients and to redefine all human distress as a species of medical illness. In 1987 the National Institute of Mental Health "discovered" that one-third of the population suffered from some sort of mental disorder. In January 1994 eight prestigious representatives of the mental health establishment published the results of a seventeen-month investigation.[57] This study reported that 48 percent of all Americans suffer from a "lifetime" mental disorder. (Although they imply that *lifetime* means a "chronic" illness, they only tell us that their subjects with a "lifetime disorder" experienced more than one episode—although not necessarily in the last twelve months.) At that time the publicity department of the American Psychiatric Association sent press releases all over the country announcing this new discovery. The *New York Times* dutifully highlighted this finding on January 14, 1994, with the headline "1 in 2 Experiences A Mental Disorder."

Although one could not tell from reading the reports in the press, a perusal of the journal report of this study makes it obvious that it was undertaken for the purpose of generating more patients for mental health professionals. Since the *Archives of General Psychiatry* is read primarily by psychiatrists and other mental health professionals, the authors did not attempt to conceal their motives. The article notes "that the majority of people with psychiatric disorders fail to obtain professional treatment" and that there is a need for "more outreach and more research on barriers to professional help-seeking." Furthermore, the authors confide to their readers that their research provides "the first nationally representative data that *can be used* in the current debate about health care policy."[58] In other words, they specifically inform their readers that this data can be used to convince the government to increase its funding of the mental health professions.[59]

I am not arguing that people do not suffer from emotional problems but rather that the mental health system has a vested interest in defining these problems as medical in nature—and thus preventing their resolution. (The story about Alice shows *how* this process works.) Through diligent effort over the last two decades the mental health system has succeeded in convincing the public that problems formerly considered "part of life"—and handled by the family or community—are in reality "psychiatric disorders" requiring professional help. Thirty years ago a claim that virtually half of the population was in need of professional help would have met with widespread incredulity.

The publication of the fourth edition of the *Diagnostic and Statistical Manual of Mental Disorders* indicates that we can expect the exacerbation of mental health professionals' tendency to medicalize all of life. As

L. J. Davis noted in the February 1997 issue of *Harper's*, "Despite the best efforts of minds great, small and sometimes insane, the riddle of the human condition has remained utterly impervious to solution. Until now. According to the *Diagnostic and Statistical Manual of Mental Disorders*, 4th edition (popularly known as the DSM IV), human life is a form of mental illness."[60]

Davis notes that each disorder, no matter how trivial, is accompanied by a billing code, enabling the therapist to fill out the relevant insurance form and receive an agreed-upon reward. Davis's skepticism is a welcome sign that at least some intellectuals are becoming suspicious of psychiatry's pseudo-scientific pretensions. He is clearly amazed that virtually every human behavior is defined as psychopathology.

> Current among the many symptoms of the deranged mind are bad writing (315.2 and its associated symptom, poor handwriting); coffee drinking, including coffee nerves (305.90), bad coffee nerves (292.89), inability to sleep after drinking too much coffee (292.89), and something that probably has something to do with coffee, although the therapist can't put his finger on it (292.90); shyness (292.80, also known as Asperger's Disorder); snobbery (301.7, subset of Anti-Social Personality Disorder); and insomnia (307.42); to say nothing of tobacco smoking, which includes both getting hooked (305.10) and going cold turkey (292.0). . . . Clumsiness is now a mental illness (315.4), so is playing video games (Malingering 362.2). So is doing just about anything "vigorously."

Davis concludes, "The pages of the DSM IV are replete with mental illnesses that have been hitherto regarded as perfectly normal behavior. The therapist is invited not merely to play God but to play lawyer—to some minds, a superior calling—and to indulge in a favorite diversion of the American legal profession known as 'recruiting a fee.' "[61]

But the horizons of the United States are not broad enough for psychiatry. In a 1990 study hailed as a landmark in modern psychiatry, Dr. James Hudson and Dr. Harrison Pope Jr. reported in the *American Journal of Psychiatry*, the official journal of the American Psychiatric Association, that they had identified a new, *worldwide* mental illness that could "emerge as one of the most widespread diseases of mankind." The authors called this global plague affective-spectrum disorder. In their research, which was supported by a grant from the National Institute of Mental Health, Pope and Hudson lumped together a range of individual "disorders"—including major depression, obsessive-compulsive disorder, attention deficit disorder with hyperactivity, and irritable bowel syndrome—in a new single category of affective-spectrum disorder. They claimed that affective-spectrum disorder "would represent one of the most prevalent diseases in the population" and that given the nature of this disorder spouses, children and other close relatives were likely to be afflicted. As a result, Pope told Joe Sharkey in a 1992 interview, affective-spectrum disorder "may affect a third of the population of the world."[62] In the meantime, American psychiatric hospital companies have been expanding abroad, opening facilities in Great Britain, Spain, Japan, Canada and other countries.[63]

The Medicalization of Life

In 1990 the anthology *Challenging the Therapeutic State: Critical Perspectives on Psychiatry and the Mental Health System*[64] was published. It included contributions from most of the major critics of the traditional paradigm in the mental health professions. The contributors hoped that it would have a major impact in the academic world. It did not. In his introduction to this anthology editor David Cohen wrote that the mental health system was involved in a large diffuse enterprise: "the medicalization of life." He stated, "The system does not seek merely to eliminate or control 'mental illness,' but to manage all aspects of social life with the aim of producing or maintaining 'mentally healthy' citizens. It constitutes one of the most encompassing projects in socio-political history, and its ideology—the medical model—now reigns supreme in the post-industrial world, explaining the innermost thoughts of individuals and shaping the social policies of nations."[65] Yet Cohen was optimistic. "I hope these [ten essays] help to chart courses toward a more humanistic, pluralistic, and non-coercive system of 'helping' those we call the 'mentally ill'—usually troubled, unhappy, and poor people who break our rules, annoy us, or threaten our values and peace of mind."[66] In the companion volume published four years later, Cohen was more pessimistic about reaching this goal. "This goal seems ever harder to reach. Medicalization/ pathologization still runs rampant."[67] He notes that despite the "considerable amount of critical scholarship during the last two decades . . . many critical authors themselves are the first to admit the impotence of their critique. In the mental health field, it seems that real 'progress' remains impossible since lay persons and professionals alike have not changed their thinking in over two centuries."[68]

There is an epistemological conflict between proponents of the medical model (I term these *medicalists*) and its critics. The former consistently conflate description and interpretation. They refuse to acknowledge that the concept of mental illness is an interpretation of data (e.g., suffering, deviant behavior) and imply or state that it is an objective description. Their success in reifying the construct of mental illness—endowing it with ontological status—is particularly remarkable in the light of two facts: one, their interpretation has failed over two centuries to produce beneficial results; two, recent developments in epistemology and studies of the history of science have demonstrated that this kind of dogmatism is philosophically untenable.[69] To put this in other terms, the majority of mental health professionals refuse to recognize that the map (the idea of mental illness) is not the territory (suffering, deviant behavior, etc.) or to acknowledge that despite their maps—or rather because of them—they have been wandering around in circles, going nowhere.

The effort to reform the mental health system, to make it more humanistic and noncoercive, as Cohen put it, has clearly failed. An astonishingly large percentage of the American population who used to be considered normal are now defined as mentally ill and subjected to debilitating, degrading and abusive intervention by professionals in the name of treatment. In the face of this failure, it is timely to remind Christians that ministering to the spiritual needs of individuals in crisis is part of the Christian mission: it never should have been delegated to secular mental health experts. The church should recognize and develop its own spiritual services, denounce the idolatry of the mental health religion—based on the worship of human ingenuity, science and professional expertise—and seek to convert individuals to a new way of life, to the way of Christ.

3

The Christian
Revolution & Its Legacy

Do not deceive yourselves. If any one of you thinks he is wise by the standards
of this age, he should become a "fool" so that he may become wise. For the
wisdom of this world is foolishness in God's sight.
1 CORINTHIANS 3:18-19

If the human race survives, future men will, I suspect, look back on our
enlightened epic as a veritable Age of Darkness. They will presumably be able
to savor the irony of this situation with more amusement than we can extract
from it. The laugh's on us. They will see that what we call "schizophrenia" was
one of the forms in which, often through quite ordinary people, the light began
to break through the cracks in our all-too-closed minds.
R. D. LAING, *THE POLITICS OF EXPERIENCE*

The prevalent belief in the Christian community is that modern
psychology is a discipline based on value-neutral scientific
expertise that significantly contributes to the enhancement of
individual welfare and to the attainment of the public good. It is evident
from the writings of Christian intellectuals and theologians who share
this belief, including those who have vigorously promulgated it, that many
of them have assiduously studied the theories of the major
twentieth-century psychologists, from Sigmund Freud to Carl Jung to
Heinz Kohut to Carl Rogers. Unfortunately there is no indication that
Christian intellectuals—perhaps with a few notable exceptions—have
made any effort to familiarize themselves with the critique of modern
psychology elaborated over the last three decades by a small but
intellectually formidable group of individuals, including the two leading

dissidents in the mental health professions, Thomas Szasz and R. D. Laing.

Yet the critique of psychology by Szasz, Laing and others is of utmost relevance for Christianity today, for at least two reasons. First, by demonstrating that psychological theories are based not on scientific inference but on cultural habits and personal choices, they implicitly undermine psychology's claim to a validity equal or superior to that of Christian revelation and witness. Second, by explicating the ethical, political and metaphysical premises or commitments upon which psychology is based, these critics enable Christians to discern where psychology conflicts with Christian values. The following cursory look at some of the ideas of Laing and Szasz is intended to inspire readers to explore in more detail the questions they raise. This I hope will eventually lead the church to liberate itself from the hegemony of psychology, to affirm its own distinctive identity as the body and bride of Christ, and to awaken its own dormant resources for effecting the healing of individuals as well as the political, social and spiritual transformation of society.

R. D. Laing and the Upside-Down World

R. D. Laing and Thomas Szasz gained their reputations as critics of the mental health system. However, they also made more general criticisms of society and of specific aspects of modern life. What most people took for granted they questioned—as if they were in this world but not of it. Given their intellectual and emotional estrangement from many of the ideas and practices within the culture, it is not surprising that they took the revolutionary step of rejecting the most fundamental dogma of the mental health system: the existence of "mental illness."

The concept of mental illness rests on the premise that the social order is natural, an ontological given, conducive to human happiness. The person who has trouble "adjusting," who is discontented, is considered to be mentally ill. Szasz stated repeatedly that *mental illness* is a metaphor that conceals the fact that the user is making a moral judgment. Laing turned the tables altogether and argued that there is something profoundly wrong, "sick" or "crazy" about the world in which we live. If this is true, then the ascription of mental illness to the alienated person is not warranted: We would not define a person who was interned in a concentration camp as mentally ill because he or she was unhappy, anxious or distressed.

Laing took the argument a step further in the mid-1960s with his contention that in many cases madness was a saner condition than normality. He reached this conclusion by first considering the state of the "normal" human being. "Humanity is estranged from its essential possibilities. This basic vision prevents us from taking any unequivocal view of the sanity of common sense, or of the madness of the so-called madman. . . . Our alienation goes to the roots. The realization of this is the essential springboard for any serious reflection on any aspect of present interhuman life."[1]

For Laing *this* world is not natural; it can provide no standard of truth, reality or justice. His argument is in accord with Christianity, which judges the world by the higher standards embodied by Jesus—whose unwavering commitment to his mission led to his crucifixion. In fact, although Laing rarely expressed himself in a Christian idiom, he was acutely aware of Christ's revolutionary opposition to the establishment of his time. In a conversation in 1985 he stated, "I'm a Christian in the sense that Christ was not crucified between two candlesticks in a cathedral. He was crucified in the town garbage heap between two thieves. In that sense I'm a Christian."[2]

St. Paul stressed the revolutionary nature of Christianity. "Do not conform any longer to the pattern of this world, but be transformed by the renewing of your mind" (Romans 12:2). "May I never boast except in the cross of our Lord Jesus Christ, through which the world has been crucified to me, and I to the world" (Galatians 6:14). "As for you, you were dead in your transgressions and sins, in which you used to live when you followed the ways of this world and of the ruler of the kingdom of the air" (Ephesians 2:1-2). Obviously, Paul did not regard adjustment to this world as a sign of spiritual well-being, that is, "mental health."

The mid-1960s was a time when the nuclear arms race had accelerated to the point where the threat of the annihilation of the human race seemed a realistic possibility and when the United States was engaged in a massive air-bombing attack on the civilian population (including women and children) of Vietnam. During the 1960s Laing was driven to doubt the sanity of a society where humans committed such acts of violence on other humans—merely because they were perceived as different and defined as the enemy.[3] Laing did not rationalize war as a natural expression of innate human aggression but interpreted it as a symptom of a particular kind of social order in which human beings had become alienated from their natural selves. Laing regarded war itself—and its acceptance as something "normal"—as evidence of the insanity of our society.

> In the last fifty years, we human beings have slaughtered by our own hands coming on for one hundred million of our species. We all live under the constant threat of total annihilation. We seem to seek death and destruction as much as life and happiness. We are as driven to kill and be killed as we are to let live and live. Only by the most outrageous violation of ourselves have we achieved our capacity to live in relative adjustment to a civilization apparently driven to its own destruction.[4]

But Laing believed there was hope—if we start by acknowledging our violence and our fears.

> Perhaps to a limited extent we can undo what has been done to us and what we have done to ourselves. Perhaps men and women were born to love one another, simply and genuinely, rather than to this travesty that we call love. . . . We have to begin by admitting and even accepting our violence, rather than blindly destroying ourselves with it, and therewith we have to realize that *we are as deeply afraid to live and to love as we are to die.*[5]

Laing tears asunder the veil of falsehoods that conceals the violence perpetrated in society by the powerful on the vulnerable: by psychiatrists on mental patients, by parents and teachers on children, by the superpowers on small, undeveloped countries. Human beings' estrangement from each other, from God, from their selves—this is the leitmotif one finds in all of Laing's works. Laing vividly paints the picture of a society which impresses on children at the earliest age—in a manner that they will never forget—that their schoolmates are their competitors in a desperate struggle for social advancement, a struggle in which one person's failure becomes the condition for another's success and vice versa. This is a society that is divided into warring camps on the basis of sex, class, race, faith, age.

Laing bemoans human beings' failure to realize the unity of the human species—an ideal to which lip service is frequently paid. But "the brotherhood of man" that is often invoked usually means group loyalty; "it seldom extends to all men. In the name of our freedom and our brotherhood we are prepared to blow up the other half of mankind, and to be blown up in turn."[6] This is an obvious reference to the arms race, which Laing viewed not merely as an ominous threat but as a potent symbol of our estrangement from each other.

Of course much of Laing's work is devoted to analyzing the estrangement between psychiatrists (and other mental health professionals) and "schizophrenics." He was keenly aware of the rift between those individuals who identified themselves as psychiatrists (or other mental health professionals) and those individuals who were defined as "mentally ill." Whereas psychiatrists attributed this rift to the alleged fact that their patients were mentally ill and thus incapable of forming relationships, Laing refused to accept this answer; he placed the burden of responsibility on psychiatrists themselves. He believed that their conviction that "schizophrenics" were not capable of forming relationships became a self-fulfilling prophecy. Psychiatrists' insistence on interpreting others' suffering as a manifestation that they were mentally defective or "schizophrenic" (i.e., essentially alien) precluded the kind of genuine communion that is sine qua non for growth, healing or transformation. A person experiencing madness or distress becomes then an object of "scientific" inquiry, a cipher to be decoded by the experts, a patient to be diagnosed and treated, not a human soul beckoning one to engage in the sacrament of communion.

It is often said that Laing discovered an alternative method for "treating schizophrenia." It would be more accurate to say that he discovered that he could be with an individual in his or her moments of madness or fear in such a way that this person—and Laing himself—emerged from the experience as a stronger and wiser person. He realized that individuals in distress—and often individuals who are not in distress but merely unusual—frequently find it difficult to conform to the *conventions* of everyday discourse. Thus he discovered a variety of unconventional ways of *being with* them. On one occasion, for example, after Laing spent an hour touching fingertips with a child who had not spoken in over a year, the child suddenly spoke.[7] It is a question not of choosing the right technique but rather of being willing to recognize one's fundamental kinship with another person. Laing welcomed the stranger—the mad person—and saw in him or her a reflection of his own self.

Communion depends upon a willingness to regard the other as one's spiritual equal. As Laing put it, "There can be no solidarity if a basic, primary, fellow human feeling of being together has been lost or is absent."[8] For Laing the failure of the psychiatrist—supposedly a master of the art of relating to other human beings—to recognize the humanity of his schizophrenic patient, to experience communion with him or her, was not merely a tragic fact but a poignant symbol of the human condition. "There can be communication without communion. This is the norm. There is very little communion in many human transactions. The greatest danger facing us, the human species, is ourselves. We are not at peace with one another. We are at strife, not in communion."[9]

Yet there are unexpected moments, glimpses of miraculous possibilities. Laing wrote in his last book,

> The new year is the biggest celebration in Scotland. . . . In Gartnavel, in the so-called "back wards," I have seen catatonic patients who hardly make a move, or utter a word or seem to notice or care about anyone or anything around them year in and year out, smile, laugh, shake hands, wish someone "a guid New Year" and even dance . . . and then by the afternoon or evening or next morning revert to their listless apathy. . . . If any drug had this effect for a few hours, even minutes, it would be world famous, and would deserve to be celebrated as much as the Scottish New Year. The intoxicant here however is not a drug, not even alcoholic spirits, but the celebration of a spirit of fellowship.[10]

Laing argued that society is structured in such a way that such fellowship is rare. He stated, "There are interfaces in the socio-economic-political structure of our society where communion is impossible or almost impossible. We are ranged on opposite sides. We are enemies, we are against each other before we meet. We are so far apart as not to recognize the other even as a human being or, if we do, only as one to be abolished immediately."[11] Laing believed that the mad were unusually sensitive people who were particularly tormented by the loss of genuine communion in society, as they were specifically disturbed by their psychiatrists' unwillingness to understand them as persons. In a lecture in 1985, he stated that schizophrenics "find it very difficult to live in the world of the interpersonal and the intrapersonal and . . . see how stupid it all is, how ugly is all is, how inexpressibly confused it all is, and yet are disregarded as crazy and mad for realizing that, and are either locked up or run away."[12]

We are not only estranged from each other, we are estranged from God. In previous eras human beings *experienced* God: faith was not a matter of intellectual assent but of trusting in the Presence that was experienced and known. Commenting on modern times, Laing states, "It seems likely that far more people in our time experience neither the presence of God, or the presence of His absence, but the absence of His presence."[13] This then is the tragedy of modern secular society: even the nostalgia for God has been lost. How then can we find our way back when we do not even have a sense of what we have lost? There is a veil between us and God that is "more like fifty feet of solid concrete. *Deus absconditus.* Or we have absconded."[14]

Thus Laing was multiply convinced that there was something essentially wrong with the world. Yet to reach this conclusion he had to have a vision or an experience of another way of being. The world need not be this way. There is a disjunction between the way things are and the way they ought to be, the way God intended them to be. Laing's assessment of our problem is largely congruent with the Christian vision (although he rarely used the Christian idiom): Our estrangement from each other and from God is the symptom of our fallenness, of our failure to live by the norms embodied by Jesus.

In such a situation the equation of madness with irrationality becomes questionable. Accordingly Laing believed that although the mad person may be confused, he or she often had an experience of the supernatural dimension of existence, of the divine, that many modern people deny even exists: "He can often be to us, even through his profound wretchedness and disintegration, the hierophant of the sacred. . . . We are distracted from our cozy security by this mad ghost who haunts us with his visions and voices which seem so senseless and of which we feel compelled to rid him, cleanse him, cure him."[15] We fail to realize that madness is potentially liberation, that it affords the possibility for the rebirth of the self. (This topic is explored in chapter five.)

When Laing says that schizophrenics have more to teach psychiatrists about the spiritual life than psychiatrists their patients, why should we be surprised? Should not Christians expect that the pariahs of the modern age have something to teach us? Our master was himself considered a pariah. What do psychiatrists, the "wise" of this age, know? Their goal is not to bring individuals into conformity with the way of Christ but rather to help them adjust to the ways of the world. But Christ told us that the way of the world and his way are in opposition.

Paul likewise said that the wisdom of this world is foolishness in God's sight (1 Corinthians 3:19). Neither Jesus nor Paul called upon individuals to adjust to *this* world. Christ paid no heed to the judgments that the Pharisees made about who was pure and who was impure, who was ready for salvation and who was deficient, who was normal and who was insane. (Jesus himself was considered insane by his family at one point.) Paul said, "Where is the wise man? Where is the scholar? Where is the philosopher of this age? Has not God made foolish the wisdom of the world?" (1 Corinthians 1:20). He goes on to say,

> Think of what you were when you were called. Not many of your were wise by human standards; not many were influential; not many were of noble birth. But God chose the foolish things of the world to shame the wise; God chose the weak things of this world to shame the strong. He chose the lowly things of this world and the despised things—and the things that are not—to nullify the things that are, so that no one may boast before him. (1 Corinthians 1:26-29)

It is easy to dismiss Laing. The issues he raises are troubling—as were the issues raised by Jesus. Laing hit a nerve when he claimed that society's pariahs, "mental patients," were more insightful about the state of the world than psychiatrists. He transgressed the boundaries of social propriety when he argued that psychiatrists were "mind police" hiding behind the façade of being objective scientists. He raised the kinds of questions that a prophet raises, and for this reason he was vilified by psychiatrists and intellectuals committed to maintaining the status quo. He refused to confine himself to the role of a mental health professional seeking to discover more effective methods to help individuals "adjust" to the world around them. He wrote, "Social adaptation to a dysfunctional society may be very dangerous,"[16] thus placing before us the task of spiritual regeneration and social reorganization. This is in fact the Christian mission. Laing provided an invaluable service to Christians and all human beings by reminding us of how far the world is from the kind of world foreshadowed by Christ, where human beings live in harmony with each other and with God.

Thomas Szasz and the Upside-Down World

Despite their differences in literary style and Szasz's vitriolic polemic against Laing's apparent espousal of communism,[17] there was considerable common ground between them. Both rejected the concept of mental illness (Szasz was the first), and both agreed that there was something profoundly wrong with our way of life. Both believed that we live in a world in which human beings regard each other as enemies, as rivals in a desperate struggle for worldly power. Both regarded the mental health system as a brutally oppressive instrument of social control that had successfully disguised itself as an association of medical specialists dedicated to the control or elimination of mental illness. Both believed that we live in a society that is governed not by the spirit of human fellowship, the "brotherhood of man," but by the law of the jungle. Szasz put it succinctly, "Loving the Other as you love yourself is the original sin, the unforgivable crime in a society dominated by the tribal ethic."[18] Although Laing and Szasz did not write as Christians, they demonstrated that the function of the mental health system is, in effect, to help individuals to adjust to a society whose way of life is contrary to the values espoused by Jesus (and to the values that are generally considered part of our Judeo-Christian ethical heritage).

Although Szasz's assessment of Laing was not entirely accurate, there were some strong points of disagreement between them. Szasz did not consider Laing's portrait of the mad person as a budding mystic or as an unwitting social critic to be insightful. Szasz believed that he was asserting the equality of all persons, including the mad, whereas Laing was romanticizing mad persons by claiming they were superior to "normal" persons.

Furthermore, Szasz rejected Laing's idea that madness was an existential crisis that presented an opportunity for a spiritual breakthrough. Laing not only asserted this, he attempted to demonstrate it by establishing an alternative asylum (Kingsley Hall) where people in crisis could experience a breakthrough instead of being inducted into careers as mental patients, as they typically were in psychiatric facilities.[19] It is here that Laing's work supplements Szasz's, and one might have expected Szasz to have relied upon it or at least to have paid tribute to Laing for attempting to prove the efficacy of a humanistic alternative to the conventional psychiatric treatment of those labeled "mentally ill."

But curiously Szasz seemed antipathetic to the idea that mad persons were in need of or entitled to any form of (voluntarily accepted) help. Instead he consistently maintained that madness was merely a form of deviation from social norms that became problematic only as a result of psychiatric interventions. This position is so at odds with the data that it led some of Szasz's critics to charge that he restricted his psychiatric practice to "neurotics" and had no experience with the more troubled persons whose rights he advocated in his books. In any case Szasz's theory of madness is incomplete because he barely acknowledges its existence—other than as a kind of deviance.[20]

In other respects Szasz's accomplishments surpassed that of Laing: in his books he develops a sophisticated historically oriented explanation of both the violence of the mental health system and of society at large. While I cannot deal adequately with this theory here, a brief description is relevant.

Szasz contends that all human societies have been based on the ritual sacrifice of human beings, the scapegoating of innocent individuals who are stigmatized and either murdered or otherwise excluded from the community.[21] While we pride ourselves on how civilized and enlightened we have become in the Western world in the past century, Szasz argues that we are as barbaric, as murderous, as bedeviled by bigotry and superstition as were our forebears. While psychiatrists view the Inquisition and the persecution of heretics as a product of a bygone age of religion and superstition, institutional psychiatry is itself a continuation of the Inquisition, according to Szasz. He writes that the labeling of persons as mentally healthy or diseased "constitutes the initial act of social validation and invalidation, pronounced by the high priest of modern, scientific religion, the psychiatrist; it justifies the expulsion of the sacrificial scapegoat, the mental patient, from the community."[22]

Like the anti-Semite, the psychiatrist is so convinced she is a warrior in a courageous battle against evil—mental illness—that she is oblivious to the harm inflicted on those whom she imagines are her beneficiaries. Szasz writes, "Because the anti-Semite fights evil, his goodness and the goodness of the society he is fighting for cannot be questioned. . . . The institutional psychiatrist treating involuntary patients is similarly engaged in a task whose goodness is so self-evident that it justifies the vilest of means. He deceives, coerces, and imprisons his victims, drugs them into stupor and shocks them into brain damage. Does this lessen the goodness of his work? Not at all. He is fighting evil."[23]

All of society bears responsibility for the persecution of mad persons. "Like all systematic popularly accepted forms of aggression, psychiatric violence is authorized, and incorporated into, important social institutions, and is sanctioned by law and tradition. . . . The State authorizes the involuntary incarceration of 'dangerous' mental patients; the family approves and makes use of the arrangement; and the medical profession, through psychiatry, administers the institution and supplies the necessary justifications for it."[24]

Scapegoating is popularly accepted because it serves a variety of social functions, including stabilizing the social order, strengthening the cohesion of the community and helping to define the identity of the group. "The scapegoat is necessary as the symbol of evil which it is convenient to cast out of the social order and, which, through its very being, confirms the remaining members of the community as good."[25] On a more general level, the process of deriving meaning for one's own life by destroying the meaning others have given to theirs (or are attempting to give to theirs) exemplifies the dynamic of what Szasz terms "existential cannibalism."[26]

By using this phrase Szasz indicates how negligibly human beings have been influenced by the noble ideals they have developed in the course of history. Yet Szasz reminds us of these ideals and encourages us to transcend our present condition. He states that "man's refusal to sacrifice scapegoats—and his willingness to recognize and bear his own and his group's situation and responsibilities in the world—would be a major step in his moral development, comparable, perhaps, to his rejection of cannibalism."[27]

What is the source of Szasz's faith that such transformation is possible? In the light of his own analysis it seems to require a process of both profound spiritual conversion and extensive political reorganization. Is this not a miracle beyond our capacity? At any rate, Szasz is quite aware of the stakes. "I believe . . . that in the rejection, or transcending, of the scapegoat principle lies the greatest moral challenge for modern man. On its resolution may hinge the fate of our species."[28]

The Christian Revolution

It is significant that Laing and Szasz, the two most prominent critics of the mental health system, were also scathing critics of society, excoriating society for its failure to live up to the Christian ideals on which it is ostensibly based.

Although these critiques failed to change the mental health system— and the fact that they were not even heeded by the church itself is evidence of its own disorientation—they were at least in part a product, as I will attempt to demonstrate, of the victory that the crucified God wrought on the cross and of the redemptive promise that Christianity still holds.

There are various attempts to account for the efficacy of Jesus' messianic work, but the *Christus Victor* model of Christ's crucifixion and resurrection best illuminates both the power and the weakness of Christianity throughout history. In the classic version of *Christus Victor* Christ gives up his life as a ransom to the devil, who held humanity in bondage. Once humanity is released from captivity, Christ tricks the devil by escaping and returning to God. Humanity has been finally freed. Even in this fanciful version the model conveys the radical nature of the opposition between Christ and the powers of this world.[29] (The modern versions of this model eliminate its anachronistic features and bring out its significance for our time.)

Throughout the New Testament there is a radical and irreconcilable opposition between the present social order—the rulers of "this age," the philosophers of "this age"—and Jesus Christ. The conflict results finally in the crucifixion of Christ. The concrete social and spiritual resistance to the Son of God led to Christ's crucifixion. St. Paul tells us that the wisdom of the rulers of this age means nothing.

> We do, however, speak a message of wisdom among the mature, but not the wisdom of this age or of the rulers of this age, who are coming to nothing. No, we speak of God's secret wisdom, a wisdom that has been hidden and that God destined for our glory before time began. *None of the rulers of this age understood it, for if they had, they would not have crucified the Lord of glory.* (1 Corinthians 2:6-8, emphasis added)

Jesus, the one truly innocent man in history, the Lamb of God, "the image of the invisible God," was condemned to die by the powers of this world. Threatened by his message, the Jewish religious establishment apprehended Christ and turned him over to the executives of the Roman Empire, who declared him an enemy of the state. At the behest of the masses who turned against Jesus, they sentenced him to death, nailed him to a cross and left him to suffer in silent loneliness and agony. Three hours later, he expired.

Jesus chose to accept without violence the death sentence passed against him. He anticipated that God would vindicate him, thus establishing the validity of his way of life and exposing the evil nature of the rulers of the world.

Had the drama ended with Jesus' death, he would have vanished from the collective memory, preserved in the historical record only as an obscure messianic pretender, and the powers of the world—the Jewish religious establishment, the imperial state, the emperor—would have remained the idols of humanity. But when the crucified Jesus was viewed in the light of his resurrection, the pretensions of the powers of the world were unmasked—for now it was apparent that they had crucified the Son of God, the Lord of glory—and the world itself was convicted of sin. Prophesying his own death Jesus said, "Now is the time for judgment on this world;

now the prince of this world will be driven out" (John 12:31). Triumphantly he proclaimed, "The prince of this world now stands condemned" (John 16:11).

Hendrik Berkhof delineates the rulers of this age who were Christ's adversaries: the scribes who crucified him in the name of Jewish law; the priests who crucified him in the name of the temple; the Pharisees who crucified him in the name of piety; Pilate who crucified Him in the name of Roman justice and law. (Berkhof omits the mob who called for Christ's death.)[30] Similarly, theologian Thomas Finger says that Christ suffered under the "corporate network of sin and evil regulated in part by the State."[31] The resurrection manifested Christ's triumph over the powers. Paul states, "Having disarmed the powers and authorities, he made a public spectacle of them, triumphing over them by the cross" (Colossians 2:15).

Berkhof explains that Christ disarmed the powers by allowing them to execute him, thus revealing in the light of his resurrection their evil tendencies.

> The weapon from which they heretofore derived their strength is struck out of their hands. This weapon was the power of illusion, their ability to convince men that they were the divine regents of the world . . . the most basic and ultimate realities . . . the gods of the world. . . . Since Christ we know that this is an illusion. . . . We are called to a higher destiny; we have higher orders to follow, and we stand under a greater Protector. . . . No Powers can separate us from God's love in Christ. . . . The Cross has disarmed them, wherever it is preached the unmasking and the disarming of the Powers takes place.[32]

The powers have been unmasked, but their reign has not completely ended. Paul continues to speak of "the present evil age" (Galatians 1:4). Precisely because the truth has been revealed, Christians must continue the work that Christ began, "For our struggle is not against flesh and blood, but against the rulers, against the authorities, against the powers of this dark world and against the spiritual forces of evil in the heavenly realms" (Ephesians 6:12). Paul assumes that the evil forces of this world are servants of even stronger demonic powers.

Christianity and Devictimization

Probably the most profound and historically illuminating version of the *Christus Victor* model has been elaborated in the last several decades by René Girard.[33] Girard may be appropriated by orthodox Christians with some caution, since aspects of his understanding of the atonement may too strongly reject certain historical models. But in today's postmodern climate of intellectual nihilism—or at best ironic pluralism—Girard's unabashed religious faith has gained him more notoriety than it has popularity. Nonetheless intellectuals have found it easier to ignore or to ridicule than to refute his powerful argument that the deepest insights of Western culture stem from biblical revelation.

According to Girard, all of human culture has been involved in a cycle of unconscious and murderous violence. At a certain point in the development of culture (due to a process that need not detain us here) a crisis ensues that evokes the specter of ultimate chaos. The group's stability and identity is threatened. A group or an individual is arbitrarily selected (usually based on the possession of characteristics that mark them as different), blamed for the dissension within the group and murdered or expelled from the group. Girard calls this process the "scapegoat mechanism" and indicates that it works unconsciously. This serves as an outlet for social frustration, stabilizes the status quo and restores the group's sense of its own righteousness.[34]

In order for the scapegoat mechanism to work, the perpetrators must actually believe in the culpability or impurity of the expelled or murdered victim(s). To protect this belief from doubt, the persecutors construct a deceptive narrative which both confirms their belief in the guilt of the victim and constitutes the basis of their identity as a group.[35]

The world has been locked in a vicious cycle of violence and victimization which continually takes on new guises and claims new victims. As Girard puts it, "The whole of human culture is based on the mythic process of conjuring away man's violence by endlessly projecting it upon new victims."[36] Christianity interrupts this process, although it does not bring it to an immediate halt—as evidenced by the violent history of the church.

Girard's faith in Christianity's redemptive powers is based on two pillars. First, it is based on the New Testament. With a power and lucidity unsurpassed in the history of civilization (and Girard would probably add of the history of divine revelation itself), the New Testament pierces the delusional system that makes scapegoating possible. The Gospels summon human beings to venture out of the cave of self-deception into the light of brighter and nobler possibilities.

A formidable coalition is arrayed against Jesus, yet it is unsuccessful in imposing its viewpoint. Girard calls Satan "that process which makes false accusations so convincing that they become the unassailable truth of entire communities."[37] By putting Jesus to death the rulers fall into a trap and the scapegoat mechanism becomes revealed. The resurrection reveals that the victim was innocent and hated without reason—Christ was the Lamb of God led to the slaughter. The persecutors' rationalization for their persecution is for the first time exposed as falsehood. The idea that the victim is always guilty is now thrown into doubt. We have now learned to identify our own innocent victims by putting them in Christ's place.[38]

The idea that God desires the sacrifice of human life as a tribute to him—a misconception that places the responsibility for violence upon God—is a projection of human violence upon God, according to Girard. He states that the "abyss" that separates the Father from the world comes from the world itself and its violence. By dying without violence (without either agreeing with his executioners and thereby sanctioning their violence, or taking a position of vengeance against them) Jesus crosses that abyss and reveals to human beings the way to salvation. This is the good news, "God is not violent. . . . The son He sends us is one with Him. The Kingdom of God is at hand."[39] The kingdom of God has nothing to do with the satanic principle of internal division and expulsion.[40]

The second pillar of Girard's faith is that of historical development. Historical development without divine intervention and revelation would have no human significance. There is a dialectic between the two, between the divine and the human, that results in "progress," to use a term that has misleading connotations when conceived in a purely secular sense. God's revelations, his sudden interruptions into history, are understood through gradual assimilation over a course of centuries. As Girard put it, "Jesus' victory is thus, in principle, achieved immediately at the moment of the Passion, but for most men it only takes shape in the course of a long history secretly controlled by the revelation."[41]

Girard finds evidence for this victory in modern history, which he believes is dominated by the consequences of the victory that was defined first by Jesus and then by Paul. He states that modern history is a process of the vindication and rehabilitation of more and more persecuted victims. New "hidden victims" of society are continually being revealed: first it was the slaves, then the lower classes, then people of different ethnic groups. Today we have become aware of the victimization of women, of handicapped people, of the young and of the old. (Girard does not mention the movement of former "mental patients.") Western history is a "turbulent, chaotic, but constantly accelerating process of devictimization that is unique in all of world history and it can be traced only to Christianity."[42]

It is remarkable that Thomas Szasz and René Girard developed strikingly similar analyses of the human dilemma and of human history with no evident awareness of each other's writings. The writings of each author both complement and parallel those of the other. Girard reveals how Christianity itself exposes the process of scapegoating, a fact that Szasz does not notice since he thinks Christ's death can be interpreted only as a propitiatory sacrifice. Szasz deconstructs the dominant social narrative in the West in the second half of the twentieth century, revealing the victims of society who have remained hidden for approximately two centuries: mental patients. (New victims include the growing population of individuals who are deceived into believing they need psychiatric treatment [see chapter one].)

Christianity and the American Revolution

The historical context of Laing's and Szasz's critique of the mental health system is the modern world described by Girard, where—for all its problems—there is an increase in the ability to detect hidden victims. What Girard failed to note, though it is implicit in his analysis, is that "devictimization" is at the same time democratization—the extension of democratic rights to groups previously excluded from the community of citizens protected by the Constitution. (For example, the enfranchisement of Blacks and women was an integral part of the process of their devictimization.)

In fact the American Revolution itself might be described as the most significant watershed in the devictimization process initiated by Christianity; it signaled (at least ideally) the end of the domination of the many by the few. From a Christian perspective in which all individuals are equal, any kind of nondemocratic government constitutes a form of victimization, an unwarranted deprivation of each individual's right to have a voice in the government of their society. The converse is also true: monarchy and other forms of nondemocratic government are a violation of individuals' rights only if all individuals are spiritually equal, as Christianity affirms them to be.

Jesus' affirmation of the equality of all human beings as children of God was the first formulation of the essential principle of democracy. It set the foundation for the American Revolution, for the revolutionary repudiation of the divine right of kings and for the establishment of a government based—in theory, at least—on the equality of all human beings in the sight of God.

Christ instructed his disciples, "You are not to be called 'Rabbi,' for you have only one Master and you are all brothers. And do not call anyone on earth 'father,' for you have one Father, and he is in heaven. . . . The greatest among you will be your servant. For whoever exalts himself will be humbled, and whoever humbles himself will be exalted" (Matthew 23:8-12). Clearly the principle of hierarchy—except that distinction between human beings and God, and human beings and animals—is radically undermined in the New Testament: it has no ontological or spiritual foundation. While certain hierarchical roles may remain, they have only a *functional* significance and are not rooted in differences of worth. Thus the only justification for leadership is that one is acting as a servant for the good of others. Obviously this claim can be used to justify oppression—a fact that Christ himself noted. However, the significant point is that Christ established a new ideal, which he commanded his disciples to embody in their own lives.

In Matthew's Gospel when the disciples ask, "Who is the greatest in the kingdom of heaven?" Christ pointed to a child and said, "I tell you the truth, unless you change and become like little children, you will never enter the kingdom of heaven. Therefore, whoever humbles himself like this child is the greatest in the kingdom of heaven" (Matthew 18:1, 3-4). The child, who occupies the lowest place in the family, becomes the model of discipleship. This saying is not merely an invitation to childlike innocence but is "a challenge to relinquish all claims of power and domination over others."[43]

Christ rejected all forms of domination over human beings. When the apostles began arguing about who among them was to be considered the greatest in the kingdom of God, Jesus rebuked them. "The kings of the Gentiles lord it over them; and those who exercise authority over them call themselves Benefactors. But you are not to be like that. Instead, the greatest among you should be like the youngest, and the one who rules like the one who serves" (Luke 22:25-26). Christ reminded them that although he was greater than they, he came as a servant.

The religion of the cross undermines the basis of hierarchy for Paul also. He admonishes his listeners to follow the example of Christ.

> Your attitude should be the same as that of Christ Jesus:
>   Who being in very nature God,
>   did not consider equality with God something to be grasped,
>   but made himself nothing,
>   taking the very nature of a servant,
>   being made in human likeness.
>   And being found in appearance as a man,
>   he humbled himself
>   and became obedient to death—
>   even death on a cross!
>   (Philippians 2:5-8)

Paul affirms the ontological equality of all men and women, their equal worth in the sight of God. This is a renunciation of the hierarchical principle that reigns in the world. But it is obvious that some individuals are superior to others in terms of talent, skills or virtues, yet Paul states that this ought not to be a source of pride, since all gifts come from God. "What do you have that you did not receive? And if you did receive it, why do you boast as though you did not?" (1 Corinthians 4:7). The strong do not have the right to rule others but are responsible for promoting their growth. "We who are strong ought to bear with the failings of the weak and not to please ourselves. Each of us should please his neighbor for his good, to build him up" (Romans 15:1-2). He reminds us that Christ died for the "weak." Furthermore, Paul tells us that Christ has given everyone in the church—even the person of low social status in society—his or her own ministry so that each can contribute to building up the body of Christ until we all reach "the fullness of Christ" (Ephesians 4:11-13).

Jesus' rejection of the doctrine of human inequality was revolutionary and unprecedented. At the time, the emperor was believed to be God's agent or representative on earth. The existential, or ontological, difference between humans and God was believed to be paralleled by the difference between monarchs and their subjects. The reverence monarchs received placed them in a category far above that of ordinary humans. Their right to rule was vested in them by God or the gods—and it certainly did not require any kind of ratification by mere human beings. Furthermore, Christians lived in a society ranked by a hierarchy of class, family, wealth and above all by whether they were Romans, foreigners or slaves. The latter were accorded a subhuman status and denied virtually all legal rights.

The Christian doctrine that all human beings are equal in the eyes of God was implicitly subversive of the divine right of emperors and monarchs. It implied that no human being had the right to rule another. In a society in which all are equal, government must be based on the consent of the governed. Many of the Christians in the first few centuries realized this and were beheaded for refusing to affirm the divinity of the Roman emperors. Clement of Alexandria declared that since God made every human being in God's image, "I would ask you, does it not seem to you monstrous that you—human beings who are God's own handiwork—should be subjected to another master, and even worse, serve a tyrant instead of God, the true king?"[44]

In the fourth century, Christians succumbed to the seduction of worldly power and accepted the patronage of Constantine; for centuries after, until the time of the American Revolution, the divine right of kings went virtually unchallenged. This was primarily because, as historian Harry Jaffa noted, "The Roman Empire founded by Caesar completely dominated the mind and imagination of Western man."[45]

Yet as Jaffa also wrote, "The connection between democracy and the ethics of [the] Judeo-Christian tradition thus understood appears ineluctable."[46] Nearly eighteen hundred years after Christ affirmed the equality of all human beings, the political implications of this connection were spelled out in the Declaration of Independence, which Christian minister and abolitionist Theodore Parker called "the American profession of faith in political Christianity."[47] The Declaration of Independence was the first application of the principles of Christianity to the organization of the political and social life of a nation.

In *The Radicalism of the American Revolution* Gordon Wood noted the negligible impact the Christian doctrine of equality had had on social and political life in the many centuries before the American Revolution. The aristocracy and gentry of the traditional monarchical society regarded the lower orders as little better than "animals." The republicanizing tendencies of eighteenth-century thinking challenged these age-old distinctions and harkened back to the Christian doctrine of the equality of human beings. Wood writes, "By assuming their inferiors had realities equal to their own, they in effect secularized the Christian belief in the equality of all souls before God."[48] While this belief may be secularized, it rests on an ontological foundation first explicated in the New Testament (although it was prefigured in the Old Testament assertion that all human beings were created in the image of God).

The disparity between America's political ideals and the actual functioning of its government need not concern us here. Parker was aware of this even as he praised the Declaration of Independence in the nineteenth century. If the mainstay of democracy is self-government, "a government of the people, by the people and for the people" (Lincoln borrowed this phrase from Parker), then it is clear that American democracy is deficient: it is more accurate to define it as an oligarchy with a façade of public participation.

Nevertheless, the democratic ideal as embodied in the Declaration of Independence and the U.S. Constitution—which include not just the right of self-government but the right of minorities and other enumerated rights—has had a regulatory effect on the American government (and other governments). In addition, it has been a source of reform movements over the centuries that have led to the extension of significant democratic rights to individuals and classes of people previously defined as inferior (e.g., blacks, women, immigrants). Furthermore, the struggle for democracy continues, nationally and internationally.

The Struggle for Democracy

The work of Thomas Szasz and R. D. Laing can be seen as the latest phase in the attempt to realize Christian and democratic ideals. René Girard has pointed out that the Greek word for "Holy Spirit" is *paraclete,* which means lawyer for the defense, for victims.[49] Thus those who act on behalf of victims are acting under the inspiration of the Holy Spirit. In the 1960s for the first time, a class of individuals who had been victimized for centuries—"mental patients," mad people, the "mentally ill"—found two powerful defenders in Szasz and Laing. The victimization of mental patients is both political and social. Politically they are deprived of the freedoms deemed by the founding documents of the United States to be the rights of all individuals. Socially the practices of psychiatry result in their exclusion from community life; their segregation in ghettos, that is, service institutions overseen by mental health personnel; and their relegation to what is essentially a permanent underclass—a caste whose social status and opportunity for social mobility is comparable to the lowest caste of untouchables in India.

Laing tended to minimize if not ignore the significance of the deprivation of mental patients' political rights and to focus on their social oppression. Szasz on the other hand might be aptly referred to as the first abolitionist of the mental patients' rights movement: while he wrote poignantly of their social oppression, he devoted most of his writing to protesting the deprivation of their democratic and Constitutional rights, primarily their involuntary confinement and "treatment" without any kind of due process, even when they have committed no crime. He explicitly invoked the Declaration of Independence, the Constitution and the American democratic tradition in general (frequently citing Jefferson, Locke, Adams and Supreme Court decisions), and he made specific demands for the extension of democratic rights *and* responsibilities (he strongly opposed the insanity defense) to mental patients. It was Szasz's work more than Laing's that inspired the mental patients' rights movement that began in the early 1970s (whose impetus was lost by 1990). The movement demanded "the end of involuntary psychiatric intervention, . . . holding that such intervention against one's will is not a form of treatment, but a violation of liberty and the right to control one's own body and mind."[50]

The former mental patients with whom I have spoken experienced these violations of their liberty to be more disturbing than the actual physical tortures imposed on them in psychiatric wards. What they found most appealing about Szasz's work was his demand that they not be excluded from the community of citizens protected by the Constitution from deprivation of liberty without due process of law. The fact that psychiatrists have the power to incarcerate and drug mental patients against their will—despite clear-cut evidence that psychiatrists have no ability to predict their danger to self or others[51]—is a glaring example of how the power of the Therapeutic State has led to the replacement of due process and thus to the erosion of fundamental rights guaranteed by the United States Constitution.[52]

In short, Thomas Szasz and the radical wing of the mental patients' rights movement agree that psychiatric theories are pseudoscientific ideologies designed to demonstrate that "mental patients" and former mental patients are inferior, and thus to justify stripping them of their rights as citizens and relegating them to a status analogous to that of African-Americans during the days of slavery. From this perspective the critique of these ideologies is a theoretical expression of the struggle for the full democratization of society and the extension of equal rights to all adult human beings.

But the story I am telling here is antithetical to the psychiatric narrative, which is about the growing problem of mental illness and the need to strengthen the power of the mental health system in order to resolve or contain this problem. The alternative narrative I am suggesting is about the gradual extension of democratic rights and responsibilities to oppressed minorities. Those who oppose this process invariably do so by invoking the alleged incompetence or inferiority of those who are subject to their power. (This is what the defenders of slavery did in the nineteenth century.)

Thomas Szasz clearly saw himself as one of the protagonists in the effort to realize democratic ideals. It is significant that he quoted Frederick Douglass in the concluding chapter of *The Manufacture of Madness*. Douglass stated in 1885 that the language of the Constitution is " 'we the people'——not we the white people, not even we the citizens, not we the privileged class, not we the high, not we the low, but we the people . . . we the human inhabitants; and if Negroes are people they are included in the benefits for which the Constitution of America was ordained and established."[53] Szasz ends this book with the exhortation that the benefits of the Constitution be extended also to the so-called "mentally ill."[54]

4

The Challenge to the Church

Overcoming Constantinianism

I have a dream that one day every valley shall be exalted, every hill and
mountain shall be made low, the rough places shall be made plain, and the
crooked places shall be made straight and the glory of the Lord will be revealed
and all flesh shall see it together.
DR. MARTIN LUTHER KING JR., "I HAVE A DREAM"

The crisis of Christianity, I am convinced, is not that it has become irrelevant
to the world—for in a way it always remains "scandal to the Jews and
foolishness to the Greeks"—but that the Kingdom of God, as value of all
values, the object of its faith, hope and love, the content of its prayer: Thy
Kingdom come! has become irrelevant to Christians themselves.
FATHER ALEXANDER SCHMEMANN, *CHURCH, WORLD, MISSION*

Although Christianity has had a positive effect on the world, as the
last chapter emphasized, the world has had an equally powerful—
and destructive—effect on the church. This explains the vexing
problem of what theologians have termed "the delay of the parousia." Both
Jesus and Paul preached that the kingdom of God was imminent. Although
Jesus stated that no man, even the Son, knew the time in which the
kingdom of God would dawn on earth, it is probable that the earliest
Christians never expected that almost two thousand years after Christ's
death and resurrection, humanity would be living under such deathly
conditions.

The history of the church has not been an unbroken, gradual ascent but in some crucial ways a deterioration from which the church has not yet recovered. Of course this is what the Protestant Reformation announced in its day, but it was the Radical Reformation[1] which accurately recognized that the "fall" of the church took place, as neo-Anabaptist John Howard Yoder put it, "at the point of that fusion of church and society, of which Constantine was the architect, Eusebius the priest, Augustine the apologete, and the crusades and the Inquisition the culmination."[2] Thus Christianity was transformed from a religion that appealed for the most part to social outcasts into the official ideology of the Roman imperial conquerors.

The church had been established to continue the messianic work of Jesus. But when the church decided to collaborate with Emperor Constantine it took on an entirely different and incompatible task: consolidating the empire and maintaining social order. Jesus had scoffed at Satan when he offered him the prospect of worldly dominion, but the church succumbed to the same temptation when Constantine, in the guise of a Christian, offered it a share in the kingdoms of the world.

Another phase in this decline took place when the leaders of the Reformation called on the rulers of their respective national states to assist them in implementing reforms. Yoder describes the outcome: "What is called 'Church' is an administrative branch of the State on the same level with the Army or Post Office. Church discipline is applied by the civil courts and police. It is assumed that there is nothing wrong with this since the true Church, being invisible, is not affected."[3]

In the twentieth century, Christianity still bears the marks of the transformation it underwent during the centuries succeeding Constantine. Even in the United States, where the church is formally independent of the state and where the church has been indispensable in promoting progressive historical change (e.g., the American Revolution, the abolition of slavery), Christianity remains denatured in several respects as a result of the changes it underwent during the Constantinian phase of its development. My discussion here will be too brief to do justice to the historical complexity of Christianity; its main purpose is to explicate my interpretation of Christianity, with an eye to understanding the church's Constantinian abdication of responsibility to the mental health establishment.

There are several prevalent (mis)interpretations today that I contend are products of the church's Constantinian turn. (These interpretations are not necessarily independent of each other, but one may imply another.) First, a prevalent interpretation, or misinterpretation, of Christianity is that it is an otherworldly, or purely spiritual, religion. Second, Christianity is often construed as apolitical. Religion and politics are believed to deal with different and incommensurable realms of experience. Third, Christianity is often fatalistic. Predestinarian interpretations have often led the church to shirk its own messianic task.[4]

A Purely Spiritual Religion?

The traditional Christian vision that salvation will involve an eschatological transformation of the earth itself—the return to paradise, the establishment of the kingdom of God on earth—is not prevalent today among Christians. This idea is and always was prominent in Eastern Christian theology—though rarely taken seriously in practice.[5] In the last few decades a number of Western theologians (such as Jürgen Moltmann, Wolfhart Pannenberg, J. Christiaan Beker and Howard Snyder) have attempted to recover the this-worldly eschatological dimension of Christianity, but their influence has not as yet had a great impact upon the culture as a whole.

For centuries we have failed to distinguish between original Christianity and Christianity as it has been shaped and revised by historical and political forces. Albert Schweitzer first shattered the composure of post-Enlightenment sensibility when he demonstrated at the beginning of the twentieth century that Jesus was (unfortunately, Schweitzer thought) an apocalyptic Jewish prophet who, as N. T. Wright put it, "dreamed the impossible dream of the kingdom bringing about the end of world history"[6] and that the early church was thoroughly eschatological.

Although Schweitzer placed responsibility for the misrepresentation of Christianity on the modernist biases of his contemporaries,[7] it is evident now that its roots lie in the Constantinian age, when the church first made an accommodation with worldly power. Monarchs believed that their reigns were divinely determined and sanctioned, and they were not likely to tolerate a worldview that held that their rule was corrupt and provisional, soon to be replaced by the perfect and incorruptible kingdom of God. Thus after the church accepted the patronage of the state, the next step in their union was "the conscious abandonment of eschatology."[8]

The idea that Christianity is purely spiritual (unlike Orthodox Judaism, which envisions material salvation) is the view articulated by most intellectuals today. There are a number of variations on this spiritualized version of Christianity, but they all eschew the idea of Christ's second coming, the conquest of death, the general resurrection and the miraculous transformation of the natural world—the kingdom of God on earth.

Rodney Clapp has observed that in evangelical Christian circles the vision of the kingdom of God has been "privatized and spiritualized." He writes, "Frequently the Kingdom is understood to be something that comes only in the individual's heart, through a one-on-One relationship with God. And salvation's fullness is anticipated to come after death, in heaven, quite apart from any life on earth."[9]

One highly influential school of liberal Protestantism in the twentieth-century[10] reinterpreted the Christian vision in "existential" categories derived from Heidegger: the kingdom of God was reduced to a state of existential authenticity within the soul of the individual believer.[11]

Given the dominance of the otherworldly interpretation of Christianity, it is certainly understandable why Jewish theologian Martin Buber criticized historic Christianity for its exclusion of earthly redemption, but it is revealing of the intellectual confusion of our century that as erudite a biblical scholar as Buber failed to discern that there is no biblical warrant for this exclusion in the Old Testament or the New Testament.[12] On the other hand, when Christian theologian G. C. Berkouwer quipped that Buber was attacking a caricature of Christianity, he ought to have acknowledged that it is a caricature accepted by many Christians themselves.

Berkouwer astutely notes that when the expectation of a new earth is denied, the very meaning of life on this earth here and now breaks down. "Carried to its logical extreme," he writes, "this concept would require denial of everything created and an evaluation of Genesis 1:1 as the least comprehensible verse in the Bible."[13] Berkouwer argues that Buber has failed to grasp the "very meaning" of the Christian proclamation: "The believer [in Christ] is called to salvation in a framework that includes the prospect of a new heaven and a new earth."[14]

Although Berkouwer's interpretation is not dominant in the Christian world today, it has a sound scriptural basis. The New Testament does *not* call the believer to place his hope in the prospect of an *otherworldly paradise*—of heaven—as a consolation for suffering in a world eternally in bondage to sin, disease and death. To both Jesus and St. Paul this world is not the way God meant it to be.

Second Peter 3:13 states, "But in keeping with his promise we are looking forward to a new heaven and a new earth, the home of righteousness." The same words are used in Revelation 21:1-2: "Then I saw a new heaven and a new earth. . . . I saw the Holy City, the new Jerusalem, coming down out of heaven from God, prepared as a bride beautifully dressed for her husband. And I heard a loud voice from the throne saying, 'Now the dwelling of God is with men, and he will live with them. They will be his people, and God himself will be with them and be their God. He will wipe every tear from their eyes. There will be no more death or mourning or crying or pain, for the old order of things has passed away.' " This of course echoes the prophecy of Isaiah 65:17-19:

> Behold, I will create
>   new heavens and a new earth.
> The former things will not be remembered,
>   nor will they come to mind.
> But be glad and rejoice forever
>   in what I will create,
> for I will create Jerusalem to be a delight
>   and its people a joy.
> I will rejoice over Jerusalem
>   and take delight in my people;
> the sound of weeping and of crying
>   will be heard in it no more.

Perhaps most significant of all is the fact that *Christianity is in its origins and essence a resurrection faith that would not have survived at all had not Christ risen from the dead.* The apostles' and Paul's affirmation of the resurrection decisively refutes Buber's belief that Christianity offers only an otherworldly salvation: it is a *this*-worldly triumph over physical mortality itself that is at the root of Christian faith.

Paul said in 1 Corinthians 15:12-14, 20, "But if it is preached that Christ has been raised from the dead, how can some of you say that there is no resurrection of the dead? If there is no resurrection of the dead, then not even Christ has been raised. And if Christ has not been raised, our preaching is useless and so is your faith. . . . But Christ has indeed been raised from the dead, the firstfruits of those who have fallen asleep." J. Christiaan Beker succinctly summarized Paul's eschatology: "God's act in Christ aims at the redemption of history and creation. Only at that time will God's promise to Israel, which is *ratified* in Christ, be *fulfilled* for God's whole creation, and only then will the faithfulness of God be fulfilled in the new order of 'righteousness,' of which Christ is the proleptic manifestation"[15] (emphasis added).

For Paul it is the mission of the church to bring God's work to completion. It does this through acting as a force of reconciliation on both a social and a cosmic level. As Howard Snyder aptly observes, "The Church is more than God's agent of evangelism or social change; it is, in submission to Christ, the agent of God's entire cosmic purpose."[16] This is the fulfillment of the prophesy in Isaiah 11:6-9,

The wolf will live with the lamb,
  the leopard will lie down with the goat,
the calf and the lion and the yearling together;
  and a little child will lead them.
The cow will feed with the bear,
  their young will lie down together,
  and the lion will eat straw like the ox.
The infant will play near the hole of the cobra,
  and the young child put his hand into the viper's nest.
They will neither harm nor destroy
  on all my holy mountain,
for the earth will be full of the knowledge of the LORD
  as the waters cover the sea.

We see here that suffering is not natural to existence; instead the principle of division and conflict—reified as the laws of nature—pits individual against individual, group against group, species against species, and alienates all creatures from God. But God restores the unity of creation through Christ, so that all creatures will dwell in paradisiacal harmony, and the laws of nature will themselves be transformed so that there will be no more suffering or destruction and "God will be all in all" (1 Corinthians 15:28 NEB).

In conclusion, the Christian vision of this-worldly cosmic redemption and transfiguration has been largely obscured over the centuries. In the twentieth century the one Christian who did more than any other person to recapture the eschatological understanding of Christianity was the Reverend Martin Luther King Jr. Not only did King view the Christian vision as one of social transformation, but unlike other Christians who participated in movements for social justice, King did not secularize the Christian message. He embraced the eschatological dimension of Christianity and appealed to the visceral yearnings for earthly redemption that had been smoldering in the souls of Black Americans for centuries, since they first appropriated the Judeo-Christian tradition during the days of slavery. The powerful messianic strain within the civil rights movement gave it a sense of élan and an irresistible momentum, which helps to explain its extraordinary success.

King and those he represented gave witness to the same truth proclaimed by Martin Buber: "The redemption must take place in the whole corporeal life. God the Creator wills to consummate nothing less than the whole of his creation."[17] Thus King demonstrated that the church is the heir of the promises made to Abraham and Israel, and is the bride of the resurrected Lord.

The mental patients' liberation movement, launched in the 1970s, protested against the same kind of invidious caste distinctions that had held down Black people—created and sustained in this case by the mental health system. However, this movement had no churches to support it and never produced leaders who combined the demands for justice and equality with the idiom of messianic Christianity. Thus it is not surprising that this movement has had negligible effect.

Historians have concluded that the vitality and willingness to sacrifice on the part of the early Christian community stemmed in large part from their sense that the redemption of the entire earth was near at hand. Recently Johann Metz has argued that the viability of Christianity depends on recovering the eschatological sensibility, with its sense of discontent with the status quo, its seemingly utopian hope, its desperate urgency and its willingness to follow Christ. This will enable the church to become again a revolutionary witness in society, to prevail against all conventional expectations and to midwife a new world.[18] Christians must appreciate the implications of this fact: only by rekindling the messianic embers within the collective imagination of the species, the hope against hope, will it be possible to motivate human beings to turn away from a sinful existence conformed to the pattern of the age and to make the kind of political, social and spiritual changes that are the prerequisites for God's final act of redemption.

Christianity as Apolitical

There is no biblical warrant for the prevalent Christian view that Christianity deals with a private, inward realm that is independent of the individual's political and social life. Historically this interpretation has enabled some church leaders and powerful laypeople to cultivate their "piety" while sanctioning or tolerating an alliance with despots. For other genuinely pious and more sincere Christians (the Franciscans and Russian monks and nuns come to mind) the depolitization of Christianity was a defensive strategy for maintaining a realm of autonomy for religious worship, a realm protected against encroachment by the autocratic state. In either case, the idea that religious practice is strictly private is a vestige of the Constantinian phase of Christianity. Insofar as it is still accepted today it justifies, among other things, the church's abdication of responsibility for the oppression of mental patients by the mental health system.

The work of God in the Old and the New Testaments is the calling and the formation of a covenanted people whose primary loyalty is to God. Obedience to God's will is a political act that is inevitably regarded as subversive in an idolatrous world. Thus it is not surprising that in the Roman Empire Jews were oppressed, Christ was crucified, and early Christians were thrown to beasts for their refusal to give allegiance to the emperor over Christ.

A recent review of all the relevant scholarly research on the historical Jesus concludes that Jesus was a social and political revolutionary determined to bring about both the liberation of Israel and the salvation of all humanity.[19] According to N.T. Wright, Jesus mounted a "social revolution" designed to prepare Israel for its role as servant in the dawning kingdom of God; Jesus exhorted his followers to act as if they were already released from exile and the kingdom of God had been inaugurated. Thus Jesus urged humans to live in accord with the ideals of equality, nonviolence, forgiveness, and reverence and love for God, that is, holiness. But Jesus was a peculiar revolutionary in that he explicitly opposed armed resistance to pagan oppression, advocating love of the enemy instead. Thus he enraged not only Rome but many within Israel itself (i.e., those committed to a war of national liberation).[20]

This does not mean of course that Christ shied away from ideological conflict. On the contrary, he actively sought it out, seeking to embody in symbolic actions his theological, political and moral differences with his opponents. Thus he entered into Jerusalem on a donkey, clearly enacting the fulfillment of messianic prophecy (Zechariah 9:9-13), and dramatically cleared the temple. He made overt the conflict between his own way and the way of the world, even to the point of provoking his own death.

The ideals articulated by Jesus and those inspired by him were embodied in their social lives. Jesus' table community included the poor, sinners, tax collectors, prostitutes. All members of Israel were welcome: women as well as men, prostitutes as well as Pharisees.[21] Following suit, the church today ought to include those labeled and outcast as "mentally ill."

Throughout the second century, Christians continued to demonstrate commitment to their ideals. They shared their money and possessions, emphasized the equality of all persons and in many cases risked death by refusing to participate in the cult of the emperor. The Christian Neo-Platonic philosopher Clement of Alexandria, for example, stated that since God created everyone is his image, "both slave and free must equally philosophize, whether male or female in sex."[22] Christians believed that by conforming to the ideal of equality in the church they were acting in accord with God's will, which was more important than conforming to the customs of Rome.

The church's willingness today to cede responsibility for the psychological well-being of its members to mental health professionals is in large part the result of a compartmentalization that stems from its Constantinian turn: the political and social dimension of life are regarded as secular, subsumed under the dominance of the state and divorced from the private-spiritual sphere. In the nineteenth and particularly in the twentieth centuries the spiritual sphere has become even more constricted. It is bifurcated into two separate realms: the psychological and the spiritual. The former is widely believed to be an important, value-neutral domain that has no relationship to one's religious convictions. The church seems to have accepted—as if there were a social contract—the idea that it ought to consign itself to ministering solely to individual spiritual needs (e.g., regularly receiving communion) and allow the self-proclaimed scientific experts in psychology—who are licensed (or "ordained") and regulated by the state—to take care of individuals' psychological needs. Almost all Christians accept that mental health professionals alone have the "scientific expertise" to help individuals with their psychological problems, which are believed to be weightier and more serious than "spiritual issues." Unfortunately, few persons realize that this distinction is entirely specious, that there is no distinctively "psychological" domain.

Christian Fatalism

Another characteristic that Christianity assumed during its Constantinian phase was the commitment to the idea that human beings have no free will in regards to salvation, that salvation or damnation is completely determined by God. It is hard to reconcile this idea with the biblical witness since the Old and the New Testaments constitute the story of God's entreaty to human beings to repent and to honor their obligations to God.

Christianity is heir to the prophetic tradition of Judaism—a religion not just of words but also of deeds. Humanity has a part to play in the drama of redemption. Humans must change their way of life so that they are able to receive the blessings of God. Some Christians believe that the only prerequisite for salvation is to acknowledge that Jesus Christ died for their sins. They do not realize that Jesus Christ demanded much more of us—to become Christlike. As Rodney Clapp points out, in the Great Commission

Jesus instructs his disciples to make disciples from all nations "and to obey everything that I have commanded you" (Matthew 28:18-20).[23] This is to say people are to be inducted into a different way of life, the way of Jesus.

The Eastern Orthodox Church has always taught that since God created human beings in his image, the process of salvation initiated by God calls for human cooperation. The twentieth-century Orthodox theologian Vladimir Lossky put it succinctly: "God does not want to impose Himself on man. He wants the answer of faith and love."[24]

Martin Buber's eloquent description of the perspective of prophetic Judaism is true also of Christianity. He wrote, "The redemption of the world is left to the power of our conversion. God has no wish for any other means of perfecting His creation than by our help. He will not reveal His Kingdom until we have laid its foundations."[25] In prophetic Judaism there is an integral relationship between our Godlike deeds in the present and God's consummation of the process of redemption. But this is also what Jesus taught—thus he demanded that we be Godlike, that we be like him.

George Eldon Ladd argued that the Jewish apocalyptic tradition—which arose after the prophetic tradition had become dormant during the most bitter period of Israel's exile—surrendered to a dualism that obscured the relationship between the present and future, between history and salvation: God no longer acts in history or attempts to influence human activity through the prophets but will be active again *only* at the end of time. Despite the influence of apocalypticism on Jesus, primarily in his vivid sense that nature was subject to supernatural influences, he rejected its distinctive dualism. Jesus recovers the prophetic tension between history and eschatology in a new and even more dynamic form. In Christ's person—and in that of his disciples, I would add—the kingdom of God is active in history, but it will be consummated by the Father only in the future. Ladd stated, "The eschatological consummation of the Kingdom is inseparable from and dependent upon what God is doing in the historical person and mission of Jesus."[26]

I would like to reformulate Ladd's statement to make it relevant for today, the era of the church. The eschatological consummation of the kingdom is inseparable from and dependent upon what God and humanity are doing in the historical association and mission of the church, the body of Christ. I do not see how one can deny this and still call oneself a Christian.

An implication of this is that the eschatological consummation depends at least in part upon the degree to which the church acts in a manner consistent with the vision and praxis of Jesus and Paul. A church that carries out inquisitions, as did both the Protestant and the Catholic churches, is hardly acting in obedience to the commandments of Jesus. If Christians begin to build on the foundations laid by God in Christ, if the church becomes the medium in which our transformation and growth can take place, if it becomes an example and light to the world, *then* the Father will consummate the process of salvation, and the kingdom in its fullness will have broken into history through the work of the church, the body of Christ. But to accomplish this work Christians must believe it is possible.

One of the reasons the church has surrendered to psychiatry is because it has largely accepted the otherworldly or spiritual interpretation of Christianity. Therefore Christians do not believe they can act as catalysts for the realization of the kingdom of God on earth. But it is clear that without the eschatological vision of the kingdom of God on earth and the sense of our own responsibility for the realization of this vision, we will not have the motivation to break with the authorities, structures and powers of "this world." In a world that is ravaged by wars, oppression, starvation, disease and death, we must dare to imagine—as the Jews did in the Old Testament and as Jesus and the early Christians did—a world where human beings will live in peace, without suffering and death. We need to envision a world where life will become a continuous act of worship and praise, sustained by an attitude of wonder, awe and gratitude to the Creator-Redeemer God who has blessed us with the miracle of life. We must now listen and heed the call of our God, who is beckoning us out of captivity into the promised land, toward his kingdom of heaven on earth.

5

The Western Shame-and-Guilt Culture & the Myth of Mental Illness

The vocabulary of psychiatric diagnosis is in fact a massive pseudo-medical justificatory rhetoric of rejection. In short, psychiatrists are the manufacturers of medical stigma, and mental hospitals are their factories for mass-producing this product. . . . Being considered or labeled mentally disordered—abnormal, crazy, mad, psychotic, sick, it matters not what variant is used—it is the most profoundly discrediting classification that can be imposed on a person today. Mental illness casts the "patient" out of our social order, just as surely as heresy casts the "witch" out of Medieval society. That, indeed, is the very purpose of stigma terms.

THOMAS SZASZ, *THE MANUFACTURE OF MADNESS*

In a previous chapter I argued that the world in which we live has no more claim to be normative—at least for Christians—than a concentration camp; thus we should not deem someone who has trouble adjusting as "mentally ill." In this chapter I will argue that the term *mental illness* reflects an anthropological perspective, a view of humanity, that is misanthropic and profoundly pessimistic.

The term *mental illness* is presented by psychiatrists as a scientific observation or description. But reflection shows that this is not the case. As an immaterial entity, the mind cannot be diseased. As psychiatrist Ron Leifer noted in his book *In the Name of Mental Health,*

If we grant that in . . . medicine the term "disease" refers to the body, to modify it with the word "mental" is at worst a mixture of logical levels called a category error, and at best it is a radical redefinition of the word "disease." Category error is an error in the use of language that, in turn, produces errors in thinking. . . . Whatever the mind may be, it is not a thing like muscles, bones and blood.[1]

With this consideration in mind we may inquire: What exactly does it mean to assert that someone is "mentally ill"?[2] In the first place it means that the mind is in a state of disorder. It falls outside the benevolent sovereignty of nature. If we examine psychoanalytic and psychiatric literature, we find an abundance of terms that denote or imply damage, defect, structural deformation or a loss of integral wholeness. The terms *mental disease* and *illness* also connote a loss of purity, as if the mind has been contaminated by a virus or bacteria. Freudians frequently state that the pathology is "deeply rooted" in someone regarded as "severely mentally ill." In other words it is at the foundation of the soul and entrenched—thus difficult if not impossible to dislodge. If it were dislodged, the soul by implication would be without a foundation.

Dispensing with metaphors, the message conveyed by the psychiatrist or psychologist to the patient is: There is something profoundly wrong with you. You are not like other human beings. The subtext is that there has been a diminishment or destruction of the "mentally ill" person's worth as a human being. It is ironic that when this message is delivered it is also usually asserted that the patient suffers from "low self-esteem"; in fact the low self-esteem is allegedly a "symptom" of the patient's "pathology." Yet what could possibly undermine a person's self-esteem more than to be told by a "scientific expert" that he or she is mentally ill?[3]

Second, the idea of mental illness implies that a breach occurred in the order of nature. At one time—perhaps at the moment of birth—the individual was well, falling within the benevolent sovereignty of nature. But then something went wrong (according to Freudian theories, the parents failed to provide good enough care), and a breach of the natural order occurred. As a result the person suffers from a "psychiatric disorder" or "psychopathology."[4]

Third, the individual has little or no freedom. (The more severe the illness, the greater the curtailment of freedom.) For the psychotic the disease is in total control. Virtually all of the patient's behaviors are deemed to be involuntary "symptoms" of a disease. It is for this reason that psychiatrists argue that the mentally ill (the "insane" in legal terms) are not responsible for criminal acts they commit.

Fourth, although there are gradations of mental illness, those suffering madness can be divided into two basic types: those who are "mentally disordered" and those who are "mentally ill." The former can be cured by psychotherapy or medication; the latter ("schizophrenics," "manic-depressives," etc.) must learn to live with their illnesses. Some "borderline personalities" can be cured, but some are too "seriously ill" to be cured.[5]

The so-called "scientific" concept of mental illness is in large part a secularization of the Augustinian interpretation of the Fall. In the *City of God* Augustine argued (and the Reformers echoed him centuries later) that God deliberately refrains from granting grace, salvation, to an undetermined number of sinners for reasons that are completely mysterious.[6] This is termed *sovereign grace,* meaning that for the chosen it is irresistible. Augustine's concept of predestination seems unfair and arbitrary, and many would argue it is in flat contradiction to the New Testament, which declares that God desires all to be saved and come to a knowledge of the truth (1 Timothy 2:4).

According to Augustine, all humans were contained in Adam and Eve and thus bear the guilt for their crime against God. Fallen humanity constitutes a "mass of perdition"[7] and deserves eternal punishment in hell. Not only are we guilty, but we are also contaminated and damaged. The damage is passed on by the semen of our ancestors, which is "shackled by the bond of death."[8] Not only "the common mass of men, but even the most Godly and righteous," Augustine wrote, are ravaged by sin and dominated by passion.[9]

Human beings have in effect lost the ability to do good—to restrain from sinning. Although all human beings deserve to suffer in hell eternally, Augustine asserts that because of God's mercy a small minority will be saved and reunited with God. Clark Pinnock writes, "It would be impossible to say how many people have cursed God and turned from God on account of this terrible misreading of the Christian story."[10]

If we look again at the psychological theory of mental illness, we see an astonishing parallel. In the first place there is an original state of perfection. Then there is the misdeed committed by the parents. The result is a diminution or destruction of the competence and worth of the child. (The one striking difference is that the child does not bear culpability for the parents' mistakes.) The child is expelled not from paradise but from the order of nature—he or she suffers from a "psychiatric disorder," from a "mental illness." Finally, in modern psychological theory (derived from Freud) there are winners and losers: a small group who can be cured of psychological problems and a larger group who must learn to live with their "psychopathology."[11]

Although Augustine elaborated his interpretation of original sin in the fifth century, it had its greatest influence in Europe between the thirteenth and the eighteenth centuries. As Jean Delumeau shows, Augustine's pessimism was darkened by that of his more morbid followers during this period. Delumeau's book documenting the emergence of a "Western guilt culture" concludes that "the debate over Original Sin and its diverse by-products—the problems of grace, free will or servitude, of predestination—came to be one of the prime obsessions of Western civilization, a concern of all people, from the theologians to the most modest peasants."[12]

Delumeau succinctly describes the elements of this guilt complex that afflicted most of humanity for centuries: "A terrible God more a judge than a father, despite the mercy with which He was almost accidentally credited; a divine justice connected to vengeance; the conviction that, despite Redemption, there would remain only a chosen few, all humanity having deserved hellfire because of Original Sin; the certainty that each sin is both insult and injury to God; the rejection of any amusement or concession to human nature, since these remove one from salvation."[13]

For centuries human beings have lived in terror that they were not among God's chosen few and therefore would be consigned by the divine Judge to suffer eternally in the fires of hell. Persons who accepted this narrative as truth believed that there was something wrong with them. In addition to being criminals as a result of original sin, they were impure, diseased. In this interpretation of original sin, Delumeau notes that sin is "an almost material substance that stains the soul."[14] Physical impurity brings about a religious and moral depravity.

It is ironic that although modern psychology tends to regard religion as anachronistic, as a superstition if not a symptom of a "neurosis," it shows a similar preoccupation with the same themes: impurity, a sense of misdeeds whose dire consequences cannot be undone (except for those of an elite), the conviction that the worth of the human person has been diminished or destroyed. There is a collective fixation of humanity on the archetypal image of the flaw.

Obviously there has been one major change dividing psychology from medieval Christendom: the individual is relieved of responsibility for the unhappy state. The human being is no longer figured most prominently as a sick criminal who has committed an unforgivable crime, but rather as a sick patient who is the victim not of her own misdeeds but of mistakes made by her parents. At any rate the majority of human beings in the Western world remain enthralled by a variation of the narrative that bedeviled humanity for centuries.

Psychiatry in the last twenty years has come up with a new variation of this narrative that appears to be more solidly based in science; that is, it claims to rest on "hard data" that the "mental illnesses" are in reality brain disorders. Although psychiatrists claim that this is a new discovery made possible by the advances of medical science, in fact we find that the same claim was made throughout most of the nineteenth century and was finally eclipsed by psychoanalytic ideas (such as the ones described above) from the 1930s to the 1960s.[15] Cohen notes that "the claim of mental illness-as-brain disease has been elevated to the status of nearly unchallengeable dogma that makes rejection of the somatic basis of schizophrenia equivalent to rejecting the somatic basis of diabetes."[16] But as Cohen and others demonstrate, this dogma is not—despite psychiatrists' unrelenting propaganda—supported by the evidence.[17]

Psychiatry's adherence to the dogma that mental illnesses are brain diseases has little to do with scientific evidence. In the early 1970s, as Peter Breggin points out in *Toxic Psychiatry*, "the American Psychiatric Association was in financial trouble. It was losing membership and its total income was $2-$4 million per year compared to its current income of over $21 million. In general, psychiatry was losing badly in the competition with psychologists, social workers, counselors, family therapists, and other non-medical professionals who charged lower fees."[18] At the same time a small group within the profession was criticizing the American Psychiatric Association's relationship with the pharmaceutical industry. In response to these criticisms the APA formed the Task Force to Study the Impact of Potential Loss of Pharmaceutical Support. The task force concluded that many local APA member organizations and various training programs would fold without drug company support.[19] Peter Breggin summarized the developments that took place:

> The floodgates of drug company influence were opened and . . . would grow wider each year. Nowadays, dozens of seminars are supported by the drug companies and the individual names of the companies are honored conspicuously with advertisements in psychiatric journals and newspapers prior to the meetings. . . .
>
> In 1980 the APA voted to encourage pharmaceutical companies to support scientific or cultural activities, rather than strictly social activities as a part of the annual meeting program. . . .
>
> Whatever function APA had ever filled as a professional organization was now superseded by its function as a political advocate for the advancement of psychiatric and pharmaceutical business interests. Continually reiterated is the conviction that only a medical or biological image can enable psychiatry to compete economically.[20]

Self-Fulfilling Prophecies

I have been arguing that one reason human beings remain convinced of the "reality" of mental illness is that we have not yet freed ourselves from "the guilt complex" Delumeau so well described. Thus most persons remain enthralled by a secularized variation of the grim narrative and misanthropic anthropology that Augustine elaborated in the *City of God*.

Furthermore, many Christians have accepted the original Augustinian anthropology. It is imperative for Christians to commit themselves to an alternative, biblically based interpretation of the Fall that seriously reckons with its disastrous consequences, while simultaneously affirming that humans retain their dignity (as beings created in the image of God) after the Fall and that the gift of salvation is offered by God to all.[21]

But there is another reason people in modern secular society remain convinced of the reality of mental illness; they believe that it is an objective, scientific concept unlike the subjective, religious concept of original sin. Psychiatrists assert that the construct of mental illness is logically inferred from the data observed.

Mental health professionals promote this kind of obscurantism because it enables them to conceal their own will to power and their commitment to a misanthropic view of humanity behind a façade of "scientific neutrality." Ultimately how one regards the human psyche or soul is a result of a philosophical *choice*—it may be based on religious revelation, but it cannot be scientifically determined or inferred from human behavior. Given the undeniable fact of human suffering, one can regard the same person either as a noble figure created in the image of God contending with the problems of life, as a contemptible sinner being punished by God for Adam and Eve's sin or as a pitiful psychiatric patient tragically afflicted by mental illness. An important point to be made here is that the interpretation one chooses will generate data that *seems* to validate it—that is, one's interpretation acts as a self-fulfilling prophecy.

Perhaps an anecdote will illustrate how the concept of mental illness becomes a self-fulfilling prophecy. It will also illustrate how data interpreted with mental illness categories are more adequately interpreted by using categories derived from the cultural understanding of the growth process. While I was working on my postdoctoral internship in 1986 (in an outpatient clinic in a lower-income area in New York City), I became increasingly aware of how degrading and destructive the medical model—with its root metaphor of mental illness—was to clients. Virtually all of the clients that consulted me were frightened that there was "something wrong" with them. The other mental health professionals they consulted consistently confirmed their fears, thus compounding their problems.

By the fourth or fifth month of my internship I had decisively rejected the medical model. I adapted a stance of what I termed "metaphysical all-rightness" and attempted to convey to my clients that there was nothing wrong with them. Since virtually every problem a client ever presented to me could be viewed as a challenge to them to become wiser or more competent in some area of their life, there was no need to construe the existence of their problem as evidence of deficiency.

By utilizing a growth model I was drawing on the positive values typically ascribed to the growth process in our culture, unlike the case of illness. Compare, for example, the difference between a physician treating a patient for cancer and parents coaching their infant toddler to walk. The mistakes and inadequacies of childhood are not considered the result of an illness nor of an inherent flaw in character.[22] Neither is the process of nurturing and educating children treated as an onerous burden parents and teachers are forced to bear. In this culture we do not regard the many obstacles children must overcome in the course of their development as an occasion for pity, pathos or disgust (feelings that mental health professionals experience when dealing with "the mentally ill").

In contrast to previous eras, today childhood is regarded as natural and children are regarded as whole beings who have not yet grown up.[23] Typically, parents and teachers—or at least "good" parents and "good" teachers—revere their children or students and exalt in their every triumph over life's challenges (e.g., the first words spoken, the first steps taken, graduation from kindergarten and so forth). Adults derive a sense of meaning and purposefulness from the process of nurturing and educating children—and young adults as well (e.g., the novice scholar writing her dissertation or her first book).[24]

The growth model is not based on a naiveté about human behavior or an ignorance about the depth and extent of human suffering. (Neither a medical model nor a growth model in themselves can adequately explain the existence of demonic evil.) This model can accommodate the fact that individuals frequently act in ways that are not conducive to their own emotional and spiritual well-being and development. (They do this as a result of ignorance, anxiety, confusion or habit.) It is not that they are mentally ill or defective; they simply do not possess the wisdom, skills or trust that would enable them to resolve the particular life challenges that confront them as individuals. As an intern, I believed the role of the therapist was not to eradicate an illness but to provide guidance, direction and emotional support to persons who are involved in a natural process of learning and growth. (As I see it now, this is—with theological modifications—the role of the church.)

Toward the end of my postdoctoral internship in 1985 I was consulted

by a client named Adam who had been diagnosed by the psychiatrist in the
clinic as having a "major depression" and "an avoidant personality disorder."
Adam was twenty-two years old and had just transferred to a school in New
York City after having spent several years in a college in Pennsylvania. In
Pennsylvania he had had a number of friends in school and had felt very much
at home. Now he was lonely, felt uncomfortable in social situations and had
no friends. This was a source not only of boredom and loneliness but of
consternation as well, because he was afraid that there was something "wrong
with him," that he was somehow defective or "mentally ill."

Had he been seen by any other therapists in the clinic, he would have
been referred back to the psychiatrist, who would have placed him on
antidepressant medication. Adam would have attended therapy at least
twice a week for months if not years to determine the source of his
depression and of his personality disorder. (Personality disorders are
believed to require years of therapy to correct.) I reassured him that there
was nothing wrong with him. I reinterpreted his problem from that of a
mental disorder to a lack of experience, social skills and shyness. I said to
him, "Social skills come with practice. You tend to be shy; you have more
difficulty making friends in the beginning. But the fact that you had a
number of friends in Pennsylvania proves that you can do so again." Since
he seemed reluctant at first to initiate any moves toward making more
friends, I "prescribed the symptoms": I suggested that he make no efforts
to make friends, that this would happen naturally when the time was right
and he was ready.

Within three weeks his depression had dissipated completely, although
he still had not made friends. When I asked him how he accounted for the
disappearance of his depression, he responded that my remarks helped
him to realize that there was really "nothing wrong" with him. We agreed
to reduce the therapy sessions from once a week to once every two
weeks—this move seemed to further bolster his self-confidence. After
several months he spontaneously and rather effortlessly made several
friends. We agreed to terminate therapy, a move that infuriated my
supervisor (a psychologist) who insisted that the original diagnosis proved
that Adam was seriously mentally ill and needed long-term therapy and
medication. The tension between us was so great that I terminated my

internship at that time, two months prematurely. I did a "followup" on Adam, approximately six months later, and he reported that he had several friends at school and was happy with his life.

I have described my interactions with Adam not because they were particularly challenging or because his story was unusually fascinating. The point is that it starkly illustrates the "therapeutic value" of merely communicating confidence to individuals—confidence in their competence and spiritual integrity. I did not see this client for more than twelve sessions, and yet the problem was entirely resolved by conveying to him that there was nothing wrong with him and that he was capable on his own—at his own tempo—of handling the challenge of life.

Unlike the mental illness model, which demeans individuals, the growth model encourages them. If a growth model were adopted in the mental health field, it would revolutionize the field within a few years. But the growth model threatens the status of mental health professionals, it undermines the caste system they have created; it would put psychiatrists and many other mental health professionals out of business as custodians of those deemed "the chronically mentally ill," and it would significantly reduce the demand for mental health professionals, resulting in a massive loss of jobs and income. That is why the growth model has no future within the mental health system—even though in a ten-year period it could save millions of individuals from spiritual and/or physical devastation or destruction.

Christian Humanism

A growth model that is based on a secularist anthropology is inadequate. Secularism does not provide an adequate foundation for an affirmation of the sanctity of the human soul.[25] If humans are, for example, merely accidental byproducts of biological and chemical processes which just happened to have occurred, if our existence is not willed by a Creator whose nature is infinite, our value is illusory, merely subjective.[26]

Christians must affirm a genuinely Christian humanism as an alternative to secular humanism—and as an alternative to the misanthropic Augustinian anthropology that has pervaded Christianity for centuries. We must repudiate the vestigial Augustinianism that prevents us from realizing our potential as human beings. A typical example of this misanthropy can be found in the book by Jim Owen, *Christian Psychology's War on God's Word*—a book that makes many astute criticisms of modern psychology. He writes, "Have you ever heard the expression 'The very sight of you makes me sick'? In a sense, this is what God is saying to all those outside of Christ. Psychologists would tell us that we would cause our children serious emotional problems if we spoke to them in such terms. Yet here is God saying that to those who do not have Christ as their Lord and Savior. . . . Thus it could be said that sin has made me so worthless in God's sight that He is repulsed by me."[27]

I find myself in unexpected agreement with "psychologists" here: it would indeed be detrimental to a child's emotional development if his or her parents were to say "the very sight of you makes me sick." But what kind of parent would feel this way? Obviously any parent on a "bad" day might feel this way, but most often they would feel that their child's being and life is precious; the child would evoke reverence rather than disgust.

Clark Pinnock has trenchantly critiqued the Augustinianism that still pervades much of evangelical Christianity, and he has eloquently affirmed the vision of God as a loving father. He writes, "The image of God as severe Judge and absolute Sovereign has driven and can still drive people to unbelief and despair. Modern atheism is often not so much a denial of the existence of God as a denial of a God like that one."[28] Pinnock and Robert Brow present as an alternative "creative love theism": human beings are "created to hear and respond to God's Word. The purpose of their existence is to enjoy fellowship with God, and sin is understood as a turning away from God's love, while salvation is a new relationship in the family of God."[29]

We must emend not only the Augustinian depiction of God as vindictive but also the Augustinian image of human beings as utterly worthless. We must affirm the worth of human beings who are created in the image of God. This image is not lost by the Fall—as both Testaments make clear (see Genesis 9:6 and James 3:9)—although it has been obscured, leading us to be lost in a labyrinth of ignorance and sin. John Stott poignantly captures the complexity of the human plight:

What we are (our self or personality identity) is partly the result of the creation (the image of God) and partly the result of the Fall (the image defaced). The self we are to deny, disown and crucify is our fallen self, everything within us that is incompatible with Jesus Christ (hence his commands, "Let him deny *himself*" and then "Let him follow *me*"). The self we are to affirm and value is our created self, everything within us that is compatible with Jesus Christ (hence his statement that if we lose ourselves by self-denial we shall find ourselves). True self-denial (the denial of our false, fallen self) is not the road to self-destruction but the road to self-discovery.[30]

If humans were purely worthless beings, as Jim Owen asserts, then the Gospels would make no sense whatsoever. The Russian Christian philosopher S. L. Frank wrote,

If man is worthless and insignificant . . . why should love for God imply love for man? On what ground can, in that case, every human personality as such be regarded as sacred? How could Christ have said that to feed the hungry, give drink to the thirsty, visit the sick—in short to satisfy even a purely material need of man as a natural being—means to manifest love for God? The sacredness of the human being as such reveals itself, in the first instance, as the sacredness of another, of "one's neighbor" and the commandment to love him and help him in his material need is based upon this. . . . True love for one's neighbor means direct awareness of something sacred and god-like in him—awareness, in virtue of which we must be considerate and attentive even to the corruptible, created vessel that contains this holiness, and respond to a man's earthly needs. But man's holy and god-like essence is the same in my neighbor as in myself. In a different way—not through concern for my earthly needs—I must respect and watch over the higher spiritual principle in me, and respect in my own self the holiness of the human personality as such.[31]

If we fail to recognize that there is something sacred and God-like in our neighbor, then we might as well be secular humanists. For the secularist the other is merely a biological being; for the Augustinian, a worthless sinner. In either case our love is either inexorably shallow—since its roots do not lie in the infinite depths of God—or delusional—since the object of our love is at best a biological creature and at worst a miserable sinner. By denigrating human beings we denigrate God, the Artist who has created us—we thus betray the Christian mission, which is based on the revelation that love is the path to salvation.

Only by regarding the other with reverence can I potentiate my ability to love him or her. Only by respecting my own holiness can I potentiate my ability to receive love. If I believe that I am a worthless sinner, then the other who regards me with love and reverence is a victim of a delusion.

It is love that enables us to see the true being—the created being—of the other. The mother who truly loves her child reveres his or her God-like innocence. The man who falls in love with a woman adores her soul and regards her body not merely as a means for "self-satisfaction, or as an end in itself, but as the outer form or garment of the divine image in man."[32] Jesus commands us to go even further: We must not only recognize and revere the God-like quality of our child or beloved but also of our enemy and of our own self. As Philip Sherrard puts it, "Unless we become conscious of our inherent nobility, as well as that of every other existing thing, we are not likely to be stirred to make even the slightest gesture capable of initiating a movement of thought and action toward the recovery of our lost spiritual vision and being."[33]

But what does this mean in terms of the theme of this book? Precisely this: no human being is mentally ill (although there are a small number who are actually brain damaged); the very idea that the mind is diseased is a reflection of an anthropological perspective that is misanthropic, pessimistic and instills in human beings self-loathing as well as contempt for others. It is a secularized version of the idea that the soul has been irreparably damaged and tainted by original sin. We can acknowledge with Stott (and with Paul) our false self, but it is also our responsibility to affirm (as both Paul and Jesus did) our authentic self that is created in the image of God.

Christians not only must affirm the sanctity of all creation, but they must create a culture—the church—in which this can be experienced. It is our task as human beings, as priests of God, to consecrate the created order, to give thanks for life and thus to affirm it both as gift and as revelation of God, as epiphany. "But you are a chosen people, a royal priesthood, a holy nation, a people belonging to God, that you may declare the praises of him who called you out of darkness into his wonderful light" (1 Peter 2:9).

It was in the liturgy and particularly in the Eucharist that Christians in the early church experienced the divine unity that will characterize humanity when the kingdom of God reigns on earth—in the Eucharist they thus had a foretaste of the eschatological salvation.

Father Alexander Schmemann, a spiritual beacon in the Orthodox Church until his death two decades ago, believed that the original understanding of the liturgy has been largely lost, and it is now misinterpreted as a means of edification or sanctification for the individual believer. The purpose of the Eucharist, as the early Christians well understood, is to manifest the church as the body of Christ; it overcomes the divisions that exist between believers and enables them to partake of a "unity from above" that imparts to each member of the congregation a deep sense of peace and joy in the Holy Spirit.[34] It is a foretaste of the kingdom of God on earth, and it thus empowers the Christian to "give unchanging and radiant testimony to the reality of the Kingdom of God."[35]

Worship is based on a sacramental understanding of the world and of human beings. It is antithetical to secularism, which bids us to live in the world "as if there were no God."[36] Fidelity to the Christian tradition requires that we realize secularism is a lie about the world and that we live in the world "seeing everything in it as a revelation of God, a sign of His presence, the joy of His coming, the call to communion with Him, the hope for fulfillment in Him."[37]

Sacramental Christianity affirms the dignity of the human being as the priest of God, as "the creature in and through which God seeks to express His own nature as spirit, personality and holiness."[38] The church must create a God-oriented culture in which humans can remove the veils that cover their hearts so that they can observe in each other's faces the undimmed reflection of the infinite glory of our Creator (2 Corinthians 3:15-18). Then we will have reached an apogee of growth unimagined by secular humanists. As one theologian put it, "To grow morally means, for Christians, to have one's whole life increasingly be conformed to the pattern of worship. To grow morally is to turn one's life into worship."[39]

6

The Church as Counterculture

I have argued that Constantinian tendencies in the church have historically led it to seek an accommodation with secular institutions
governed by norms antithetical to those of Christianity. With the
separation of church and state it may seem that the church has regained
its autonomy. But this is not entirely true—I have examined some of the
vestiges of the church's Constantinian phase in previous chapters. I want
to emphasize that while Christianity is no longer directly used (at least
not typically) to justify the power of monarchs or the state, the church
does give moral and spiritual sanction to agencies of social control that
act under the mantle of the modern state religion of "mental health." This
is because with the decline of the monarchy other forces have assumed
the task of maintaining social order. As Ron Leifer states, "The arbitrary
authority to classify and control people, taken away from the absolute
monarch by the democratic revolution, has now been granted to the
alienist [i.e., psychiatrist]."[1]

How can Christianity become again, as it was in the beginning, a force
subversive to the deployment of arbitrary power and to the subordination
of human beings to an unjust caste system (disguised today as merito-
cratic)? How can it become an agency of democratization?

In this chapter I will examine the alternative to the Constantinian
strategy that has been proposed by theorists and heirs of the Radical
Reformation. I believe that the general strategy they propose gives us clues

as to what stance Christians ought to take toward the mental health system as well as toward other dominant social institutions.

The New Israel

What form should the Christian mission now take? How should the church position itself in relation to the late twentieth-century world? I have previously discussed the mistaken notion that religion pertains to the purely spiritual realm. An increasingly popular variant of this accommodationist stance is more avowedly Constantinian: it seeks to transform the culture by becoming part of it and by collaborating with the state either to support its policies or to attempt to push them to the "right" or to the "left."

The mainline Protestant denominations have endorsed what Rodney Clapp and Stanley Hauerwas characterize as a kind of liberal Constantinianism. The church here is indistinguishable from the liberal wing of the Democratic party. It is "the dull exponent of conventional secular political ideas with a vaguely religious tint."[2] Right-wing Christians have a different social agenda but essentially the same strategy. Hauerwas is also critical of the religious right for its frequently jingoistic celebration of nationalism and its willingness to justify U.S. military crusades in the name of the professed ideals of the nation-state. Thus both left and right want to maintain Christendom "wherein the Church justifies itself as a helpful, if sometimes complaining, prop for the state."[3]

The most viable alternative to the Constantinian model of the church is the countercultural model. For the sake of simplicity I will term it Anabaptist, since its adherents either are Anabaptist or have been strongly influenced by that tradition. (A strong argument could be made, as indicated above, that this was the original Christian model held by Jesus and Paul.) The Anabaptists argue that the Constantinian model shifts its focus between the individual and the state—both of which it tends to fetishize—and overlooks the distinctive role of the Christian community as the instrument of the kingdom of God.

The most influential advocate of liberal Constantinianism is H. Richard Niebuhr, whose book *Christ and Culture* is widely regarded as definitive. The main problem, Clapp argues, is that within his frame of reference it is impossible to "imagine or enact" the church as a "distinctive theologically formed . . . culture," a nation unto itself (the New Israel); rather the church must relegate itself to the role of bringing "an individualized abstracted 'ethico-religious' system to culture."[4]

The Anabaptist position is not nonpolitical, as Niebuhr and others have charged. In the first place, its goal explicitly includes political and social change. Second, it does not reject all involvement in the dominant institutions of society, only that kind of involvement that is incompatible with Christian principles. What critics of the Anabaptists fail to see is that the countercultural strategy is based above all on the conviction that "the primary social structure through which the Gospel works to change other structures is that of the Christian community."[5]

Thus the church's first task is to *be* the church, to be that community faithful to the way of Jesus, to the kingdom of God, to be a new *polis* (to use one of Hauerwas's favorite phrases). The creation of a viable Christian community is not a *substitute* for missionary activity but the *precondition* for it. As Charles Scriven puts it, the church must be both an "alternative society" and a "transformative example"[6]—"the light of the world," "a city on the hill." The church then must become the vanguard of the new order that establishes "beachheads" (to use Beker's term) of the kingdom of God in the enemy camp, in "this world."[7]

Anabaptist theologian Thomas Finger explains in a very concrete manner the way in which the church can transform the world. The church must provide visions of alternative ways in which life can be lived, and it must then make them "actual possibilities in which people are invited to participate."[8] The church can have the most powerful transformative effect upon the world not by helping its "present structures to function better" but by presenting it with new alternative possibilities which conform to the Christian ideal of the kingdom of God on earth. These alternative models can break through the world's "systemic blindness and initiate social changes which might never have occurred otherwise."[9]

Only when Christians live wholly in the light of the "age to come" can the world be overcome and the kingdom of God take shape as a "recognizable and concretely possible option."[10] The church's missionary efforts must be "rooted in groups committed to living wholly in light of the *New Age*, inaugurated by Jesus Christ."[11] Only then can it authentically call individuals and institutions to live in the same reality.[12]

This model requires that the church create alternatives to the mental health system insofar as it conflicts with Christian principles (e.g., alternatives to mental hospitals and psychiatric wards). The goal of these alternative structures is twofold: to help individuals resolve their crises and to facilitate their eventual incorporation into the church, as a counterculture to the world. (Some individuals will choose not to become Christians. They should be offered this option, but they should not be coerced.) The countercultural model is not compatible with the church's present policy of deferring responsibility for the care of individuals experiencing distress or crises to secular mental health experts.

The premise underlying this practice strikes me as completely schizophrenic: mental health professionals are more qualified to take care of individuals' emotional or "clinical" needs, whereas the church can take care of their "spiritual" needs.[13] While the individual is seeing a mental health professional to resolve her emotional problems, a minister or priest typically will tell her that she is welcome to attend church services in order to meet her spiritual needs. If the individual is in severe distress she will have to wait until she is released from the psychiatric ward of the hospital to have her spiritual needs satisfied—unless of course the psychiatric authorities believe that she is "healthy" enough to offer her a pass to attend church.

The Myth of Professional Expertise

Mental health professionals have succeeded in convincing the public that as a result of years of training they possess special expertise that makes them uniquely qualified to help people with emotional problems. Consequently, most Christians believe it would be unethical to encroach upon the territory of the mental health scientist-professional.

The research belies the professionals' claims of scientific expertise. In 1977 Mary L. Smith and Gene V. Glass published an article in *American Psychologist* that summarized the results of 375 studies of psychotherapy. Although they concluded that therapy was effective, they also discovered that the therapist's credentials—Ph.D., M.D. or no advanced degree—and experience were *unrelated* to the efficacy of therapy.[14] Psychologist Robyn Dawes reevaluated these studies and other studies in 1979 and came to the same conclusion: "Although therapy is effective in eliminating symptoms, the credentials and experience of the therapist don't matter."[15]

Since this result is unpleasant for professionals who underwent years of postgraduate training and postdoctoral experience for licensing and who would like to restrict the practice of therapy to those who are licensed, many attempts have been made since the Smith and Glass article was first published to disprove their findings. These attempts have failed, and Dawes's conclusion remains valid. Psychologist Jerome Frank also acknowledged "the inability of scientific research to demonstrate conclusively that professional psychotherapists produce results sufficiently better than those of non-professionals."[16]

Another significant finding is that all forms of therapy are equally effective. Morris Parloff, former chief of the psycho-social treatment research branch of the National Institute of Mental Health stated, "Nearly five hundred rigorously controlled studies have shown with almost monotonous regularity that all forms of psychological treatment . . . are comparably effective."[17]

The obvious interpretation of this finding is that nonspecific factors independent of any particular form of therapy—or of nonprofessional human relationships—account for the beneficial changes. Research studies and common sense indicate that the two most salient nonspecific factors are the interpersonal qualities of the counselor and the arousal of positive expectations, as in the placebo effect. Research has consistently shown that therapists who are perceived as warm, empathic and genuine are more likely to produce positive changes in their clients. Martin and Deirdre Bobgan note, "All of these factors are at play in all effective human relationships. None of these factors require psychological training, psychological techniques, psychological degrees, or psychological licensing."[18]

It should be noted that the studies reviewed above made no attempt to assess the potentially adverse effects of therapy on the percentage of clients who did not improve. Furthermore, the conditions of these studies minimize the possibility of adverse effects as the vast majority of outcome studies were done in academic settings, where treatment is closely monitored, guided by well-designed procedures and reviewed by supervisors. Thus they are subject to "quality control" that is not available to the large majority of individuals who are treated in clinics. Second, these studies specifically excluded the kinds of clients that therapists have the most destructive effect on: those deemed "mentally ill." Third, the studies were done within narrow parameters: they obviously did not attempt to assess the overall effect of psychotherapy upon a society in which it has been embraced as a panacea for all social ills.

Nonetheless, the implications of these studies are profound: they call into question the very nature of the therapeutic enterprise and undermine the credibility of the mental health system's program for the betterment of society. The research demonstrates unequivocally that psychology—while promoting idolatry of science, of which it claims to be an exemplar—has no scientific foundation. A highly educated, "scientifically trained" and licensed psychotherapist is no more likely to be an effective agent of change than an amateur with no training whatsoever.

The Psychological Seduction of Christianity

It is not surprising that the mental health industry has made no policy changes as a result of these findings. It is however disappointing, if not surprising, that the church has not been emboldened by these conclusions to assert its own distinctive identity as an agent for social and spiritual transformation. Rather than daring to follow in the path of its Lord, summoning individuals into the salvific community, the church seeks to enhance its worldly glamor and acceptance by pursuing an alliance with Big Brother—the mental health system. Has the church forgotten yet again as it often has throughout history that our Lord himself was despised and crucified?

If not, then why has the church ignored the warnings of prophets such as Martin and Deirdre Bobgan? In *Psychoheresy: The Psychological Seduction of Christianity* they document the tendency of Christians to be intimidated from counseling—helping—individuals due to their lack of psychological training. Based on years of experience in the Christian evangelical community, the Bobgans conclude, "The most respected advice among Christians for problems of living is to 'get some counseling' and by this they mean professional psychological counseling."[19] Psychologists repeatedly tell pastors, including psychologically trained pastors, to refer individuals in distress to trained professionals. As one professor of psychology at a Christian college put it in 1983, "The pastor should be taught how to assemble a list of professionals in his community who will serve his parishioners well."[20] The Bobgans give several examples of this attitude among pastors; they state that they could multiply examples of "the referral principle" but decided not to bore the reader since "every one knows that the Church has become one gigantic referral service."[21]

The Bobgans document that the church not only refers troubled individuals to mental health professionals but, smitten by their power, it also seeks to emulate them, woo them and is ready to sacrifice its own identity in holy matrimony. An article in the *Christian Research Journal* corroborates this point:

> Churches, Bible colleges and seminaries, Christian speakers, and Christian publishers across the country are promoting mental health programs to help Christians solve their personal problems and find personal fulfillment. Many Christian educational institutions have added psychology classes and majors, and some even have Masters and Ph.D. programs in psychology. Twelve Step programs patterned after Alcoholics Anonymous (AA) have been adapted by churches to address almost any kind of persistent personal problem, from obesity to "spiritual" addictions. Some churches offer a personality evaluation with membership forms to ensure that new members have their emotional and mental health needs met in addition to their spiritual needs. There are even study Bibles designed especially for people "in recovery." Indeed, some Christians argue that inclusion of psychological principles and teachings into a biblical counseling setting is the only way to provide competent mental health care to Christians.[22]

Unfortunately there are few voices like the Bobgans' in the wilderness of Christianity today. Despite the growing destructiveness of the mental health system and the undeniable evidence that the credentials of mental health professionals are not reflective of specialized competence, Christians continue to turn to Freudians, Jungians and Rogerian-trained therapists.

The Church as Counterculture

There is a sharp contrast between the Christian cult of the scientific expert and Jesus' practice. Jesus did not defer to the "experts" of his own time. People who sought to be accepted in Christ's community included tax collectors, prostitutes, sinners of all varieties, outcasts, misfits and individuals who were regarded as "impure" in a manner analogous to the way mental patients are today. Like mental patients they were exiles not merely in the sense that Israel was in exile but from their own communities. Jesus invited them to his table, into his community, to his party celebrating the kingdom of God. Neither he nor Paul said to them, "First go back to the Pharisees to be purified, and then come back to me and I will take care of your spiritual needs." The means of purification were open to them in principle within the existing sacrificial system.[23] Jesus offered the blessings of the kingdom of God "outside the official structures, to all the wrong people, on His own authority."[24]

It is a tragic comment on the strength of Constantinianism in the church today that it is ready to so severely undermine its own authority by giving its endorsement to "official structures" that exist for the purpose of stabilizing a corrupt social order. The church can not build a strong distinctive counterculture in this fashion.

The church should also recognize that its own culture is antithetical to that of the world: it anticipates the kingdom of God. The church belongs to the age to come and is the agent of this world's conversion. As I have emphasized throughout this book, church culture is—or ought to be—distinctive and different in two salient respects: it is democratic, and it is sacramental. As argued in chapter five, worship restores to human beings "the opportunity to look on the world as it truly is"[25]—as the epiphany of God. This can have a healing and transformative effect on an individual who has trouble adjusting to a modern secular culture.

John Howard Yoder has noted that Paul's democratic model of church ministry was eclipsed in the course of history. Yoder emphasized that Paul in Ephesians uses the term "the fullness of Christ" to describe a new mode of group relationships in which every member of a body has a distinctly identifiable, divinely validated and empowered role; every member has his or her own ministry: "It was he who gave some to be apostles, some to be prophets, some to be evangelists, and some to be pastors and teachers, . . . so that the body of Christ may be built up until we all reach unity in the faith and in the knowledge of the Son of God . . . to the whole measure of the fullness of Christ" (Ephesians 4:11-13). Paul in 1 Corinthians says literally that to *every* member "the manifestation of the Spirit is given for the common good" (1 Corinthians 12:7). This obviously includes individuals who are today labeled "mentally ill" as well as those individuals with genuine (i.e., physical) handicaps.

Furthermore every Christian is endowed with the responsibility and dignity of being a priest of God, called upon to consecrate all of creation. "You are a chosen people, a royal priesthood, a holy nation, a people belonging to God, that you may declare the praises of him who called you out of darkness into his wonderful light" (1 Peter 2:9).

In *The Politics of Experience* Laing uses an illuminating metaphor.[26] He states that a formation of flying planes may be observed from an ideal vantage point on the ground. One plane appears to be out of formation, but *the whole formation may be off course.* The plane that is out of formation may appear abnormal, bad or mad from the point of view of the formation, but the formation itself may be bad or mad from the point of view of the ideally situated observer. The plane that is out of formation may be more on course than the formation itself is.[27] Laing states that the out-of-formation criterion is the clinical positivist criterion, whereas the off-course criterion is the ontological. From our perspective we can say that the off-course criterion is the Christian criterion.

From the Christian perspective we know the formation—this world—is off course. The church itself is—at its best—*out of formation but on course.* The professional psychologist may or may not help a client get back into formation but is neither inclined nor likely to help that person get back on course. *It is the role of the church to help individuals get into the church's formation*—its own countercultural community—*and thus both in formation and on course.*

7

The Mental Patient
as Exile & as
Christian Initiate

It is clear that culture may value and make socially available even highly unstable
human types. If it chooses to treat their peculiarities as the most valued variants in
human behavior, the individuals in question will rise to the occasion and perform
their social roles without reference to the ideas of the usual types who can make
social adjustments and those who cannot. Those who function inadequately in
any society are not those with certain fixed "abnormal" traits, but may well be
those whose responses have received no support in the institutions of their
culture. The weakness of these aberrants is in great measure illusory. It springs not
from the fact that they are lacking in necessary vigor, but that they are individuals
whose native responses are not reaffirmed by society. They are as Sapir phrases it,
"alienated from an impossible world."
RUTH BENEDICT

Until this point in seeking to expose the falsehoods of the mental
system, I have frequently appealed to the reader's common sense:
for example, most people would readily agree with me that the
psychologists who decided to hospitalize children because they were
irritable and blamed adults for their problems were not acting in these
children's best interest. In order to be persuasive in this chapter, however,
I need to appeal to the *un*common sense of the reader. This is because the
cultural myths surrounding the idea of mental illness have been developed
and sustained over centuries, are deeply entrenched in the popular
imagination, are powerfully reinforced by a massive public relations
campaign by the mental health industry and in quite specific ways actually

provide a sense of security for individuals in uncertain times when society is plagued by numerous social problems and conflicts.[1] It is also because the few critics of the mental health system who have been inclined to take their argument outside of academic journals have not been provided the kind of access to the media granted to professionals with more mainstream views.

In order to disabuse readers of the belief in the existence and chronicity of "schizophrenia," I will need to draw attention to facts they are probably not aware of, such as the data from non-Western cultures. Above all I want to examine the practices of the mental health system that frequently are not attended to by individuals drawing conclusions about the "mentally ill." When focusing exclusively on the experiences and behavior of "mental patients," common sense concludes that these are sufficiently explained by the construct of "mental illness." The picture begins to look totally different when one's focus is broadened. Theodore Sarbin and Jay Mancuso have argued that the myth of mental illness is sustained and *can be sustained* only by an arbitrary narrowing of one's vision—by the failure to utilize a "contextualist model."[2]

Sociologist Erving Goffman used a contextualist model when he observed the behavior of mental health professionals in psychiatric wards. From his investigation conducted in the early 1960s, Goffman concluded that incarcerated and vulnerable individuals in mental hospitals were in effect inducted into "careers" as chronic mental patients.[3] The effects of even a short stay in a psychiatric facility can be profound. This is not to deny that an individual may be in great pain before he is even brought to the attention of mental health professionals. However, as R. D. Laing once responded to a critic, "If I was feeling vulnerable or confused or terrified, I think the last place I would want to be would be one of those mental hospitals. That would be like the Aztec Indians rushing into the mouths of the Spanish cannon hoping for deliverance."[4]

It is my contention that in large part the practices of psychiatry result in the transformation of individual crises into chronic, lifelong problems.[5] My argument is supported by the voluminous literature on "experimenter bias" which proves that "an experimenter's expectations can strongly bias the performance of his subjects by means of cues so subtle that neither experimenter nor subject need be aware of them."[6] Mental patients are not merely given subtle cues: virtually all of them are told by every mental health professional they consult that they have a chronic mental illness. Clearly mental health professionals have low expectations for psychiatrically labeled individuals, expectations which powerfully influence their clients' ability to "perform" in life. Jay Haley, a family therapist who effectively helps schizophrenics and who had a training program for professionals, wrote,

> The main reason I dropped the term "schizophrenia" is that it so handicapped the teaching of therapy, I found it almost impossible to persuade psychiatric residents—or social workers, since they follow the lead of psychiatrists—to expect a "schizophrenic" to become normal. They would hesitate when they should have pushed for normal behavior, and the family would hesitate because the expert did so. Soon everyone was treating the "patient" like a defective person, and therapy failed.[7]

Jerome Frank in his review of the literature on therapist-patient relations wrote, "A therapist cannot avoid biasing his patient's performance in accordance with his own expectations."[8] He added that the therapist's influence is heightened not only by his or her role and status but also by an attitude of concern and the patient's vulnerability. The implication of this is that the more strongly bonded the former mental patient is with his therapist—who almost always has low expectations of mental patients—the more likely he is to maintain his career as a professional mental patient.

The Degradation and Segregation of Mental Patients

In 1970 Thomas Szasz observed that the labeling of persons as mentally healthy or diseased "constitutes the initial act of validation and invalidation, pronounced by the high priest of modern, scientific religion, the psychiatrist; it justifies the expulsion of the sacrificial scapegoat, the mental patient, from the community."[9] The segregation of mental patients from genuine community life leads to their spiritual if not their physical destruction.

One remarkable fact that is well attested to by a plethora of evidence[10] is the healing and transformative effect of communities on the lives of individuals. I will qualify a previous statement by noting here that this is true even in the fallen world. Perhaps this is because any genuine community, one based on the affirmation of all members—even when it is not eschatologically oriented—anticipates in some way (e.g., in actualizing democratic values) the new order, the kingdom of God.

Few individuals would claim that the plight of the "mentally ill" has improved over the last several decades—every day urban dwellers notice many disturbed individuals talking to themselves in public or cursing invisible demons. In order to evade responsibility for their own failure in this regard, psychiatrists invented a mythology that has become received wisdom over the last two decades. They claim that in the 1960s when mental patients were emptied out of state mental hospitals professionals made an effort to integrate them into the community. (The only element of truth in this assertion is that at the time a number of mental health professionals advocated such a policy.) According to this mythology this process, termed *deinstitutionalization,* failed because of the chronicity of mental illness.

Because psychiatrists found an army of credulous journalists, their official version of reality was readily disseminated to the public in the past decade. A number of journalists charged that deinstitutionalization was essentially a policy change implemented because of the influence of Thomas Szasz, R. D. Laing and Erving Goffman. Supposedly their ideas had such an impact on mental health professionals that they decided institutionalization was not therapeutic. They discharged the "mentally ill" from state mental hospitals into the community.[11]

The fact of the matter is that the emptying of state institutions did not take place because of Thomas Szasz or R. D. Laing, who have been alternatively viciously attacked or unceremoniously ignored by psychiatry. It took place for economic reasons: "because the state couldn't afford to provide lifetime care for a huge and growing chronic case load inside enormous, crumbling hospitals built in the nineteenth century, which proved to be extremely expensive to run at twentieth-century prices."[12] As historian Andrew Scull put it, the emptying of the state mental hospitals was in response to a "broad expanse of social [federal] welfare programs, growing fiscal pressure on the states, and the opportunity to transfer costs away from the state budget."[13]

Nor did deinstitutionalization take place because newly discovered neuroleptic drugs "cured" mental illnesses. Johnson wrote: "The idea that psychotropic medication caused deinstitutionalization is really part of a carefully tended mystique the companies who hold the drugs' patents have worked hard to develop on their products behalf."[14] In actuality although the "antipsychotic" drugs were introduced in the early 1950s, the state mental hospital census did not decline dramatically until after 1965.[15]

The fact of the matter is deinstitutionalization never took place. What occurred was a process Szasz aptly termed *transinstitutionalization:* transfering individuals from state mental hospitals "into *de facto* psychiatric facilities that are not called 'mental' or 'hospitals.'. . . Deinstitutionalization is simply a new fashion in mental health care, consisting of storing unwanted persons in dwellings not called 'mental hospitals' but, nevertheless, treating them as if they were mental patients who required life-long psychiatric supervision."[16] Here they are sequestered from the community in "halfway houses" (*halfway* is a euphemism, since virtually none of them make the implied transition to ordinary life), day treatment centers, group homes and group residences, subject to lifelong psychiatric supervision, kept on debilitating psychiatric "medication" and socialized to conform to the norms of *institutionalized* life—not to the community. These patients are told repeatedly by various mental health professionals that they have chronic mental illnesses which requires continuous "medical treatment"—that is, injection of neuroleptic drugs termed *medication*—and supervision.

Scull, who goes out of his way to make it clear that he rejects the "romantic nonsense"[17] propounded by Szasz and others, nevertheless arrives at a conclusion similar to that of Szasz regarding the effects of deinstitutionalization. "It is only an illusion that patients who are placed in boarding or family care homes are in the community. . . . These facilities are for the most part like small, long-term state hospital wards, isolated from the community. . . . One is overcome by the depressing atmosphere not because of the physical appearance of the boarding home, but because of the passivity, isolation, and inactivity of the residents. . . . Little effort is directed toward social and vocational rehabilitation."[18] Patients are however typically supervised by mental health personnel who ensure that they take their "medication" and make regular visits to their psychiatrists.

Mental health professionals labored to integrate the patients into the new service institutions—and discouraged their integration into the community. Communities are usually persuaded by human service advocates that "mental patients" *need* to be surrounded by mental health personnel in order to survive. Therefore they should be removed from community life in order to receive special services in special places under the guidance of professional experts. Thus former mental patients typically spend their mornings, afternoons or evenings in day-treatment centers with other patients—under the close supervision of mental health personnel. John McKnight aptly stated that labeled people live surrounded by a "forest" of services that separate them from the community.[19]

Long-term institutionalization tends to produce chronic mental patients, people whose socialization skills have atrophied and whose sense of self-esteem has been so undermined that even if an opportunity arose, it would be difficult for them to adjust to community life. The mental patient becomes accustomed to relationships with professionals that resemble those between parents and children. The professional often feels a genuine compassion for the patient, but as it is for a person of putatively inferior status or worth, it is tainted by a sense of disdain or condescension. The mental patient regards professionals as persons of greater worth and competence than themselves. In order not to be overwhelmed by a variety of fears (in particular the fear stoked by professionals of becoming "psychotic" again and having to be rehospitalized), the patient needs the repeated reassurance of professionals. Unlike the typical parent-child relationship, the patient rarely outgrows his or her childlike dependency on the professional.

Madness in the Streets: Psychiatric Myths

Although deinstitutionalization never took place, it must be acknowledged that at least as formulated by its more idealistic proponents—the social and vocational rehabilitation of patients and their reintegration into the community—it was a good idea. Although psychiatrists' intentions were influenced by economic factors and status factors (e.g., the desire to find employment outside of the dismal and low-prestige state mental hospital), some backed the movement in good faith. As one proponent put it, "By bringing [the mentally ill] back into the community, by enlisting the good will and the desire to serve, the ability to understand which is found in every neighborhood, we shall meet the challenge which such groups of persons present, and at the same time ease the financial burden of their confinement in fixed institutions."[20]

As I have said, deinstitutionalization never occurred. Nevertheless, apologists for psychiatrists argued that it had taken place and that it was a total failure that could have been foreseen from the beginning, and should not have been undertaken at all. From the perspective of Rael Jean Isaac and Virginia Armat a conspiracy involving R. D. Laing, Thomas Szasz, Peter Breggin and a small group of radical ex-mental patients succeeded in severely undermining the power of psychiatrists to impose their treatments upon mental patients. Their premise is that psychiatric power is uniformly benevolent and psychiatric treatments are uniformly successful.[21] This premise flies in the face of the facts. But the facts never disturb the promoters of psychiatry. No matter how destructive psychiatric treatments are, no matter how miserable the plight of mental patients, the argument is made that their plight would be far worse if the power of psychiatrists were restrained to any degree. Thus the failures of the mental health system are used as an argument for investing even more power in mental health professionals.

Isaac and Armat's argument is quite ironic. On the one hand they view "schizophrenia" as a chronic disease that renders individuals so helpless that they are unable to cook for themselves, maintain minimal personal hygiene, care for housing or manage money.[22] Schizophrenics, they tell us, are vulnerable, helpless, bizarre and sometimes dangerous and uncontrollable. On the other hand the book is in part a vigorous polemic against the former mental patients—virtually all of whom were diagnosed as chronic schizophrenics by their psychiatrists—who banded together with civil libertarian lawyers and dissident psychiatrists to form a movement against psychiatric coercion. The authors note that due to the "talent and vigor of its leaders"[23] the mental patients movement was able to outwit their powerful psychiatric foes and prevent them from forcing their allegedly beneficial treatments on patients who did not want them. (I will argue that the their success was much more limited.)

The question that the authors dare not consider is that if "schizophrenia" is a chronic, disabling illness, how were these mental patients able to inflict such a severe blow on their much stronger (allegedly emotionally but unquestionably financially and socially) adversary? If the authors' thesis were correct—that schizophrenia is a disabling illness that gets worse without coercive psychiatric treatment—there would not be a mental patients movement to oppose. The very existence of such a movement proves that those "mental patients" who are willing to resist the myths of psychiatry and engage in activities that increase their sense of self-worth and responsibility are able to overcome the so-called chronicity of their disease and can become powerful leaders in a movement for social change—this is the case whether or not one thinks that this movement is misguided in some or all of its tactics and goals.

So is homelessness a product of deinstitutionalization, as Isaac and Armat and countless journalists in the 1990s have stated? This argument strains credibility considering the fact that the emptying of state mental hospitals began in the late 1950s and was completed in the 1960s, whereas homelessness became a major problem only in the 1980s. Ex-mental patients were a minority of those individuals squeezed out by the housing policies implemented in the 1970s and 1980s that led to the destruction of low-income housing. In New York City, for example, the number of people living in single room occupancy hotels (SROs), which house many former mental patients, declined from 100,000 in 1965 to less than 20,000 in 1986.[24]

A superficial examination may support the claim of Isaac and Armat that the influence of psychiatrists has been curbed. For example, during the 1960s and 1970s most states enacted due process laws that made a judicial hearing a condition for confinement in a psychiatric facility. However, this judicial protection has little de facto value insofar as most judges defer to the opinion of the hospital psychiatrist, who virtually always deems the patient a danger to himself or others. In 1989 more than 51 percent of admissions to state and county mental hospitals were involuntary (and noncriminal).[25] However, in principle at least the courts have for the most part recognized that the rules of due process must apply to people in danger of being incarcerated in mental hospitals. They have thus acted in accord with the principles upon which the Bill of Rights is based and have aroused the indignation of others who prefer instead the benevolent despotism of the mental health system.

In 1978 the U. S. Supreme Court in *Addington v. Texas* affirmed the right to liberty of the mental patient. Chief Justice Warren Burger wrote,

> This court repeatedly has recognized that civil commitment for any purpose constitutes a significant deprivation of liberty that requires due process protection. . . . Moreover it is indisputable that involuntary commitment to a mental hospital . . . can engender adverse social consequences to the individual. Whether we label this phenomena "stigma" or choose to call it something else is less important than we recognize that it can occur and that it can have a very significant impact on the individual.[26]

The judge also astutely noted,

> At one time or another every person exhibits some abnormal behavior which might be perceived by some as symptomatic of a mental or emotional disorder, but which is in fact within a range of conduct that is generally acceptable. Obviously, such behavior is no basis for compelled treatment and surely none for confinement. . . . Loss of liberty calls for showing that the individual suffers from something more serious than is demonstrated by idiosyncratic behavior.[27]

By the Court's standards there is no basis for compelled treatment of the overwhelming majority of people under the supervision of mental health personnel today.

The supporters of psychiatric totalitarianism have not been successful in their drive to reincarcerate former mental patients in state mental hospitals. However, they have succeeded in their lobbying efforts to induce over half of the states in the country to enact laws enabling judges at the behest of psychiatrists to compel individuals to submit to "outpatient treatment," including the forced ingestion of toxic psychotropic drugs.

Most judges defer to the "expertise" of the psychiatrist, who is an avid proponent of these drugs.

The Dubious Miracle: Psychiatric Drugs

Another myth promulgated by psychiatry is that neuroleptic drugs are the treatment of choice for schizophrenia and that patients refuse to take them because they are so irrational that they have a resistance to getting better. Patients who do not want to take neuroleptic medication are said to be "treatment resistant."

I will start by noting a few relevant facts. It is acknowledged by virtually all psychiatric researchers that the following neurotoxic effects are produced by antipsychotic medication (neuroleptic drugs): Parkinsonism, encephalitis, akathisia, neuroleptic malignant syndrome, tardive dementia and tardive dyskinesia (TD). Limitations of space preclude a discussion of all these side effects. According to a 1986 study in the *American Journal of Psychiatry*, the most serious is the neuroleptic malignant syndrome, which has a prevalence of 2.4 percent among neuroleptic drug users and a mortality rate of 20 to 30 percent among those individuals afflicted.[28] Probably the neurological disorder that is most prevalent and most often discussed in psychiatric literature is tardive dyskinesia, a frequently irreversible disease that usually begins with uncontrollable movements of the face including the tongue, lips, mouth and cheeks. The hands, feet, arms and legs can be involved. The movements include writhing contortions, tics, spasms and tremors. Even mild cases are often grossly disfiguring and embarrassing to patients.

According to "Tardive Dyskinesia: A Task Force Report of the American Psychiatric Association,"[29] approximately 20 percent of patients receiving chronic neuroleptic treatment developed tardive dyskinesia. This figure is an understatement, because it does not take into account cases of tardive dyskinesia that are masked, which according to the study cited by the American Psychiatric Association constituted an additional 12 to 34 percent. This means the overall prevalence rate of tardive dyskinesia among neuroleptic drug users ranges from 30 to 57 percent.[30] Estimates of the number of individuals affected in America range from half a million to several million.[31] It is by all accounts a widespread epidemic.

Akathisia occurs in an estimated 45 percent of patients who are given neuroleptics (even on a short-term basis). Akathisia is an extreme restlessness that often causes mental patients to pace back and forth. (Frequently, observers incorrectly attribute their pacing to mental illness.) Jack Henry Abbott, a prisoner in a federal penitentiary who was given the drugs, poignantly described this symptom. "The drugs turn your nerves in upon yourself. . . . The pain grinds *into your fiber*. . . . You ache with restlessness so you feel you have to walk, to pace. And then as soon as you start pacing, the opposite occurs to you; you must *sit and rest*, back and forth, up and down you go in pain you cannot locate; in such wretched anxiety you are overwhelmed."[32]

The public has been led to believe by psychiatrists that the purpose of "antipsychotics" is to reduce the suffering of "schizophrenics" and other psychotics, to help them to get better, if not to fully recover. Yet a review of the psychiatric journals published at the time neuroleptic drugs were first introduced reveals that this was not the goal the drugs were intended to achieve. Psychiatrists Heinz Lehmann and G. E. Hanrahan wrote in 1954, "The aim is to produce a state of motor retardation, emotional indifference, somnolence and the dose must be increased accordingly as tolerance develops. After the first week of treatment, the patient remains retarded but less sleepy."[33] In another article published shortly after, Lehmann described chlorpromazine (the first neuroleptic used) as a "pharmacological substitute for lobotomy."[34] Also in 1954 a British psychiatrist wrote in the *Journal of Mental Science*, "Patients responding well to the drug have developed an attitude of indifference both to the surroundings and to their symptoms best characterized by the current phrase 'couldn't care less.' "[35]

The loss of initiative, the depression of motivation, the blunting of emotions, the impairment of the patient's ability to reason and think abstractly—these were readily observable effects of neuroleptics that were acknowledged in the 1950s by the psychiatrists who used and promoted the drugs; many noted their similarity to the effects of frontal lobotomy. Yet since mental patients were regarded as hopeless cases, psychiatrists felt no compunction about using such "treatments." The drugs were valued for their ability to make patients docile and easy to warehouse in state mental institutions.[36]

Peter Breggin worked as a volunteer in these hospitals in the 1950s, when neuroleptic drugs were introduced. He wrote, "The patients continued to live in relative squalor and degradation with nothing to occupy their time, but now they were easier to manage and especially easy to ignore. It became possible to forget that no human services, not even companionship, were being offered to them. Thus, the major tranquilizers solved the state mental hospital management problems as no other 'treatment' had done. They created robot-like inmates able to respond to simple commands, but like surgical lobotomy patients, relatively unable to resist or to initiate spontaneous conduct."[37]

Although the same kinds of drugs are still used by psychiatrists, today only their critics are outspoken about the lobotomy-like effects. Dr. Peter Sterling, a brain research expert at the University of Pennsylvania Medical School, wrote in 1979, "The blunting of consciousness, motivation and the inability to solve problems under the influence of [neuroleptics] resembles nothing so much as the effect of frontal lobotomy."[38] The majority of psychiatrists profess that their purpose is to mitigate or ameliorate the symptoms of psychosis. Thus they are described typically as "antipsychotic medication." Yet as Breggin has documented, "The drugs produce their effects independently of the presence or absence of any biological or psychological disorder. They have the same pacifying, subduing effect on normal individuals and, indeed, on animals."[39]

The side effects not only are destructive in and of themselves, but they can also impede patients' recovery in a variety of ways. First, their effect on cognition and motivation makes it difficult if not impossible for patients to learn new skills, such as a job would require. Second, cosmetically disfiguring akathisia and tardive dyskinesia mark individuals as "mental patients," thus making it more difficult for them to be reintegrated into the community. Third, taking "medication" constitutes a ritual of self-degradation that reinforces patients' sense of identity as "schizophrenics" or "manic-depressives," that is, their identity as defined by the psychiatrists.

Thus the mental patient is exercising good judgment when she shows a disinclination to take neuroleptic drugs. However, psychiatrists attribute this reluctance to the irrationality of the patient. In fact, the concept of the "noncompliant" or "treatment-resistant" patient used by psychiatrists is based on a blatant denial of the harmfulness of neuroleptic drugs. It implies that the patient is so sick, so irrational that she refuses to comply with the treatment that will make her better. On the contrary, neuroleptic treatment frequently makes patients feel worse. They have very good reasons for their reluctance to comply with this treatment.

For their own irrational or self-serving reasons, psychiatrists will rarely acknowledge to their patients the tragic facts about neuroleptic "medication." Numerous patients have reported to me that psychiatrists dismissed their complaints about the side effects of medication, minimized the seriousness of the problem and frequently told them that these effects were not caused by the medication but by the patient's mental illness. Furthermore, a study published by the American Psychiatric Association in 1988 concluded that, "even when informed consent about psychiatric treatment is seriously pursued, patients are provided little information about the side effects. When side effects are mentioned, tardive dyskinesia is frequently not among those named."[40] Although courts ruled repeatedly in the 1980s that failure to inform the patient of the risk of TD were instances of negligent practice, my own experience in talking to thousands of former mental patients is that psychiatrists virtually never discuss with patients the danger of tardive dyskinesia.

When patients refuse to succumb to psychiatrists' pressure to take neuroleptics, professionals frequently summon the coercive power of the state to force patients to comply with treatment. The right to due process is meaningless here because the courts virtually always defer to the expert opinion of the psychiatrist that the patient is in need of "medication." In many states, forcing the patient to submit to injections of brain-damaging drugs has been accepted by the courts as the protection of the patients' "right to treatment," which is said to override their right to liberty. Furthermore, patients living in halfway houses or other psychiatric facilities are usually threatened with eviction if they do not take antipsychotic medication.[41]

It is psychiatry's intention to use its powers to force more and more patients to take neuroleptic drugs. The American Psychiatric Association Task Force Report on tardive dyskinesia was unequivocal: neuroleptic drugs are the treatment of choice for schizophrenia despite their side effects.[42]

The main flaw of the numerous psychiatric studies that have been done supporting the use of neuroleptic drugs is that only one criterion is used to assess its effects: rate of rehospitalization.[43] The evidence does seem to indicate that neuroleptics somewhat reduce the rate of rehospitalization compared to that of individuals receiving a placebo.

This does not, however, reveal much about the quality of a person's life. It was the same argument that was made for lobotomies in the 1940s and 1950s: lobotomized patients were able to leave the hospitals and return home to their families. (Approximately fifty thousand lobotomies were performed in the United States.) The American Psychiatric Task Force Report reviewed numerous studies that concluded that rehospitalization was reduced by neuroleptic drugs. Not one study cited in the Task Force Report utilized any other measure of success, such as social integration and employment.[44] Furthermore, not one study compared neuroleptics to any treatment other than placebos or no treatment at all.

I have helped many former mental patients to wean themselves off neuroleptic drugs (sometimes with the cooperation of a psychiatrist) and go on to lead "normal" lives, returning to work or school. I have talked to several hundred individuals who have had psychotic breakdowns and have subsequently remained symptom free and off psychiatric medication for five to fifteen years at the present time. My last book, *Madness, Heresy and the Rumor of Angels,* recounts in detail the story of seven individuals who completely recovered from "schizophrenia" and have not taken medication in over twelve years.

Furthermore, as David Cohen notes, "Considerable evidence from controlled, random-assignment studies clearly shows that *given the proper social environment,* most newly identified 'schizophrenics' can be treated successfully with little or no psychotropic medication. Moreover, open studies demonstrate consistently that these types of social environments can be successfully adapted for use with veteran clients."[45] Furthermore, some studies have indicated that mild sedatives such as Diazephan were as effective in sedating clients as the more toxic antipsychotic medications.[46]

Yet the American Psychiatric Association has consistently ignored this data and persistently pushed destructive psychiatric drugs that cause permanent brain damage and make it virtually impossible for individuals to lead "normal" lives.

Psychosis as Baptism

Our view of "mental illness" begins to appear very different if we dare to see it as an opportunity for spiritual growth. As noted above I have argued in a previous book that what the mental health system regards as a "schizophrenic episode" may very well be a manifestation of the readiness of the individual to assume a new spiritual identity.[47]

Repeatedly St. Paul referred to the process of becoming a disciple of Christ as a death-rebirth experience. The new self arises from the ashes of the old. "For through the law I died to the law so that I might live for God. I have been crucified with Christ and I no longer live, but Christ lives in me." (Galatians 2:19-20) In Ephesians 4:22-24 Paul wrote, "You were taught, with regard to your former way of life, to put off your old self, which is being corrupted by its deceitful desires; to be made new in the attitude of your minds; and to put on the new self, created to be like God in true righteousness and holiness."

Frequently the individual labeled "schizophrenic" is undergoing a severe personality crisis, a disintegration of the personality that makes possible the re-creation of the self. This was first noted by R. D. Laing in *The Politics of Experience*: "Madness need not be all breakdown. It may also be breakthrough. It is potentially liberation and renewal as well as enslavement and existential death."[48] Although Laing eschewed Christian terminology in *The Politics of Experience,* his description is remarkably similar to that of Paul, "True sanity entails in one way or another the dissolution of the normal ego, that false self competently adjusted to our alienated social reality . . . and through this death a rebirth, and the eventual re-establishment of a new kind of ego-functioning, the ego now being the servant of the divine, no longer its betrayer."[49]

The disintegration of the self is frequently the precondition for the assumption of a new, more spiritually developed identity. It is the practices of the mental health system that convert the potential Christian initiate (or the Buddhist initiate or shaman) into a chronic mental patient. This contention is further corroborated by anthropological data. In "Shamans

and Acute Schizophrenia"[51] Julian Silverman compared the initiatory
ordeal typically experienced by the novice shaman to what psychiatrists
term a "schizophrenic episode." He concludes,

> Significant differences between acute schizophrenics and shamans
> are not found in the sequence of underlying psychological events
> which define their abnormal experience. . . . One major difference
> is emphasized—a difference in the degree of cultural acceptance of
> a unique resolution of a basic life crisis. In primitive cultures in
> which such a unique life crisis resolution is tolerated, the abnormal
> experience (shamanism) is typically beneficial to the individual
> cognitively and affectively; the shaman is regarded as one with
> expanded consciousness. In a culture that does not provide
> referential guides for comprehending this kind of crisis experience,
> the individual "schizophrenic" typically undergoes an intensification
> of the suffering over and above his initial anxieties.[51]

The investigation of shamanism is illuminating: whereas personality
disintegration was interpreted in premodern societies as the prelude to
reintegration and as a sign that a person was called upon to assume a
leadership position in his or her culture, in modern society it is interpreted
as a symptom of a chronic disorder. The implications of this are staggering.
Yesterday's shaman is today's chronic schizophrenic! The kind of person
who in a bygone era would have been initiated into the vocation of shaman,
medicine man, spiritual healer, is now likely to be initiated into the role
of tragic-victim-of-the-most-serious-mental-illness-known-to-modern-
civilization.

Some readers will find this statement offensive. They will object by
pointing to the obvious fact that most "schizophrenic episodes" bring little
redemptive light into patients' lives. But this is exactly my point: In the
kind of cultures examined by Silverman, the phase of personality disintegration ultimately had a positive beneficial experience. Mental illness
professionals regard these experiences wholly as negative and thus are
unable to help patients make the transition from spiritual death to spiritual
rebirth. That is why psychotic episodes usually fail to bring redemptive
opportunity into patients' lives. That is also why it is imperative that the

church provide asylums for individuals undergoing psychotic episodes and thus give them the opportunity to be spiritually reborn. If the church—which consists of disciples of the *crucified* and *risen* Christ—cannot take seriously the idea of a spiritual death and spiritual rebirth, it is unlikely that any other organization will.

The great philosopher of religion and student of shamanism Mircea Eliade also wrote that the disintegration of the personality was a precondition for the assumption of the new identity of the shaman: "The true knowledge, that which is conveyed by the myths and the symbols, is accessible only in the course of, or following upon, the process of spiritual regeneration realized by initiatory death and resurrection. . . . The future shaman, before becoming a wise man, must first know madness and go down into darkness."[52]

I will give one contemporary illustration of this process. In my previous book I described the story of a woman in her early twenties who made a transition from a homosexual lifestyle to a heterosexual orientation in a brief period of time. Before her psychotic breakdowns she had begun to believe that her homosexuality had become a façade that she felt compelled to maintain because of peer pressure. In her last psychotic episode what was clearly at stake was her sense of personal identity. She told me, "I felt as if I was going to unravel to the point where there was no I." I speculated to myself that the sense of a future ripe with new possibilities caused and demanded this divestiture of self. This was analogous to the shamanic experience. Eliade has written, "The initiatory death repeats this exemplary return to chaos in order to make possible the renewal of the cosmogony; that is to prepare for the new birth."[53] He notes that this often involves a total disintegration of the personality. In other words, my subject had undergone a kind of initiatory death as a transition to another mode of being. To use Eliade's words, she underwent "a trial indispensable to regeneration; that is to the beginning of a new life."[54]

If we extrapolate from this data it is clear that just as the disintegration of the personality, that is, psychosis, was typically the precondition for becoming a shaman, so it could well be the initial phase—for many people, to one degree or another—in the death of our old self and the resurrection (note that Eliade uses the same term as St. Paul) of the new self formed in the likeness of Christ. Yet the individual experiencing a profound crisis of this kind who goes to a minister for help will invariably be referred to a mental health professional.

What a terrible abdication of duty for Christians. At the moment of our greatest opportunity, when the individual is ready to make the transformation to a completely different mode of existence, to be reborn in the Spirit, we abandon them to mental health professionals who above all else are determined to prevent this spiritual rebirth from occurring. If the church is to become a vital force for social and spiritual transformation it must reach out to individuals in their times of crisis.

8

The Restoration of the
Authority of the Church

Professionalism has undermined the church's autonomy from dominant social institutions and compromised its ability to act as a prophetic critic of the social order. Thus, with the exception of the Bobgans, the most perceptive critics of the deleterious affect of the mental health professions on the vitality of community and participatory democracy have not identified themselves as Christians. One such critic is William Schambra, a conservative inspired by the work of Robert Nesbitt, who calls for a "new citizenship" whose goal is "the reconstruction of civil society and the return of America to the self-governing republic described by Alexis de Tocqueville and envisioned by the Founding Fathers."[1] Schambra believes that this new citizenship will need to roll back "the incursions of the therapeutic state into the every day lives of Americans by challenging the political hegemony of the 'helping' and 'caring' professions and bureaucracies. This requires dramatizing their status as entrenched corrupt special interests more concerned about advancing narrow ideological agendas and protecting political prerogatives than about the public."[2]

At the other end of the political spectrum the late Christopher Lasch reached a similar conclusion. In Lasch's book *The Revolt of the Elites and the Betrayal of Democracy,* he criticized the transformation of the United States from a self-governing republic where "even the humbler members of society" had "access to the knowledge and cultivation" required for active citizenship to a "therapeutic state" ruled by managerial elites increasingly insulated by their culture and lifestyle from the concerns of the rest of the people.[3] Denouncing "the reign of specialized expertise,"[4] he asked "Is it really necessary to point out at this late date, that public policies based on a therapeutic model have failed miserably over and over again? Far from promoting self-respect, they have created a nation of dependents. . . . The professionalization of compassion . . . institutionalizes inequality."[5]

James Hillman, a Jungian psychologist for several decades, stopped practicing therapy about seven years ago. He became disturbed by the effects of what he terms the "therapeutic ideology," which leads people to believe that the source of all their problems, resulting from events of the past, lies within them. He believes that this obscures the political nature of human existence. He argues that the "recovery movement" has become a national obsession as millions of people get together to commiserate with each other about their common victimhood as children of alcoholics, as food addicts, as recovering alcoholics, as "codependents," that is, as people who regard their need for other people as an addiction to be repeatedly examined and conquered—ironically with the help of other people! Hillman says "For everyone to sit around a room because they're fat—I don't know if that's a way a civilization can continue." He suggests as an alternative, "Suppose we begin seeing ourselves not as patients, but as citizens."[6]

Wendy Kaminer is similarly critical of the recovery movement in her book *I'm Dysfunctional, You're Dysfunctional.* She states, "With the rise of a personal development movement centered around victimization, victimology can fairly be called a study of our culture." She questions, "What are the political implications of a mass movement that counsels surrender of will and submission to a higher power describing almost everyone as hapless victims of familial abuse? . . . The notion of selfhood that emerges from recovery (the most vulgarized renditions of salvation by grace, positive thinking, and mind cure) is essentially more conducive to totalitarianism than democracy."[7]

Paul Piccone and his colleagues at *Telos* journal have developed a sophisticated critique of the welfare state and pseudodemocratic modes of New Class domination. Federal intervention has less to do with securing equal rights for everyone "than with the implementation of a New Class agenda of securing the privileges of middle-class intellectuals running state agencies and bureaucracies at the expense of an increasingly clientized populace."[8] *Telos* was founded in the late 1960s by Piccone as a "new left" journal; Piccone now maintains that the distinction between "left" and "right" is meaningless, and advocates for a renewed "populism" uniting all individuals favoring "local autonomy, fiscal austerity and participatory forms of democracy."[9]

Mental health professionals and other self-help gurus prey upon feelings of existential deficiency that I believe are vestiges of the Augustinian anthropology which has helped mold our culture. One psychologist who had been in therapy for twenty years herself wrote, "While I was in therapy I enjoyed the attention my therapist provided me. . . . I became addicted to this attention, and to keep it, I remained in the role of the dependent one, needing validation and almost by definition feeling insufficient. I pathologized myself to remain in treatment."[10]

John McKnight argues that the welfare state and the ideology of professionalism are the primary obstacle to the reconstitution of communities and the reconstruction of democracy in the United States. He writes, "The enemy is not poverty, sickness and disease. The enemy is a set of interests that need dependency masked by service."[11] Along with Lasch, McKnight regards the definition of social problems in medical terms as the prerequisites for stripping individuals of their citizenship and permanently relegating them to an inferior caste of clients. Whatever resources or services they are then "entitled to" cannot compensate for this degradation. He succinctly describes the therapeutic ideology as follows: "(1) The basic problem is you, (2) the resolution of your problem is my professional control, and (3) my control is your help."[12]

McKnight rejects "the therapeutic vision" which sees "the well-being of individuals as growing from an environment composed of professionals and their services. It envisions a world where there is a professional to meet every need and where the fee to secure each professional service is a right."[13] The only genuine solution, McKnight argues, is the realization of the "community vision," which requires "the conversion of clients to citizens."[14] The community vision seeks to relocate power from the centralized and professionally dominated service system to "neighborhood associations," which range from local churches to the neighborhood taverns, where two centuries ago "some of the most basic discussions about the formation of the government of the United States and its Constitution occurred."[15]

The community vision seeks to provide every citizen, no matter how fallible, the opportunity to participate as a political equal with other citizens in the process of community decision-making and neighborhood-building. It seeks to "recommunalize" exiled and psychiatrically labeled individuals. "It sees the community associations as contexts in which to create and locate jobs, provide opportunities for recreation of multiple friendships, and become the political defender of the right of labeled people to be free from exile [from the community]."[16]

It is ironic and tragic that at a time when advanced social thinkers such as Lasch and McKnight have critiqued the pretensions of psychology and exposed the dangerously antidemocratic nature of the helping professions that the church underestimates the resources of its own salvific community and opts for professionalism over democracy. At a time when the research published by mental health professionals themselves can not validate the efficacy of their training, even within their own narrow terms, the church vacillates between the ideals of Christ and the ideals of Freud or Jung and is seduced by the prospect of becoming yet another growth industry.

What Should Christians Do?
What does this mean for the church? To spell out all its implications would require another book. Let me briefly note several directions in which I believe the church should move.

In the first place, Christians should stop regarding mental health professionals as scientifically trained specialists uniquely suited to help individuals deal with life's problems. These disciples of the mental health religion equate adjustment to a world inimical to Christian values with spiritual well-being (i.e., "mental health"). The focus of their idolatrous worship is science, and the state and higher education ordain a caste of specialists who ostensibly have power to impart to those who receive their sacraments (e.g., long-term psychotherapy) the salvific blessings of science: the restoration of their mental health, the remediation of their damaged psyches and the ability to adjust to a profane, secular, undemo-cratic society.

Psychology and the Christian psychology movement constitute obsta-cles to the development of the body of Christ. They create an artificial hierarchy of the expert over the client and discourage Christians from ministering to each other. At the slightest feeling of discomfort mental health professionals inside and outside the church encourage Christians to seek the help of professionals. "At its best psychotherapy is rent-a-friend, but usually it's rent-a-service. . . . A true friend in Christ is of far greater value than a paid psychotherapist or paid biblical counselor, not only because the love is freely given, but also because the love is biblically given in a biblical setting: the body of Christ."[17] Thus it strengthens the body of Christ, the Christian community, and makes it more cohesive.

The danger is that the equality and interdependence of all members of the body of Christ will be replaced by "one-up" long-term dependency relationships between subordinate counselees and more powerful profes-sionals. While I do not think it is always practical to insist, as the Bobgans do, that fees never be charged for services (there are people at a less mature or crisis phase of spiritual development who may need more time than can be given without some kind of financial remuneration), it is imperative that Christian ministers and counselors stop promoting long-term rela-tionships with "professionals" and start encouraging Christian disciples to minister to each other. The goal should be to build up the Christian community, not to create another industry committed to the maximization of profit. Furthermore I heartily endorse the Bobgans' recommendation that the biblical counseling movement discontinue all counseling centers that operate *outside* a church[18]—and are thus not accountable to any church.

The Church's Responsibility for Resolving the Crisis of the Modern Secular World

As I have emphasized, the church has a particular responsibility to those individuals who are made permanent pariahs by the mental health system: "the severely mentally ill." Just as Christ felt a particular responsibility to the victims of the religious establishment of his time, so the church today has a heightened responsibility to the victims of the dominant religious establishment of the modern age, the mental health system.

Let me put it this way: I have no doubt that if Jesus were to return and be examined by a panel of psychiatrists or psychologists, they would determine unanimously that he suffered from a severe mental illness. Within their own limited frame of reference there is no other way of making sense of Jesus' metaphysical understanding and claims about himself and the world. Thus the choice before us is clear: we judge Christ by the standards of the mental health system or the mental health system by the standards of Christ. If we choose the latter course, the mental health system stands condemned, and we do not need to observe its taboos or its ritual proscriptions and prescriptions. The church should immediately establish asylums—places of retreat, healing and transformation—for individuals who are undergoing spiritual crises, that is, the "seriously mentally ill." By doing this the church will be violating the greatest taboo of the mental health system: it will be encroaching upon the most treasured domain of mental health professionals and daring to challenge its most fundamental dogma, that "mental illness" is a severe organic and/or mental disorder that must be treated by a team of highly trained and experienced professionals.

If the church takes on this challenge, it can expect massive opposition by mental health professionals and the support of the few dissident mental health professionals who have had the courage to publicly expose the spiritual and physical damage inflicted on mental patients by the mental health system. While a physician (not necessarily or even preferably a psychiatrist) should be on hand in such Christian asylums to prescribe tranquilizers (*not* neuroleptics) in the case of severe distress, the rest of the staff need not be—preferably are not—trained or certified professionals. It would be helpful if they have had some experience working with mad persons, but it is essential that they feel comfortable doing so and are unencumbered by the usual prejudices that are prevalent in society about "mental patients."

Since I believe that the majority of individuals labeled "psychotic" are suffering identity crises, I regard this as an optimal time for them to be initiated into new identities as disciples of Christ. Obviously this opportunity should be *offered,* not coerced. In my experience what mental patients need—but almost never find in a mental hospital—is the opportunity to talk to someone about their experiences, both traumatic and spiritual, without being treated in a judgmental manner, that is, without these experiences being defined as symptoms of their deep pathology. There is no reason to regard altered states of consciousness as detrimental to the soul's growth. On the contrary, it is often the most bizarre and unusual experiences that lead to the enrichment of the personality. As long as the "patients"—potential disciples of Christ—can maintain nondisruptive behavior, they should be invited to participate in the liturgical and sacramental life of the church, ranging from attending daily worship services to partaking in table fellowship at the homes of church members.

The question may arise whether the evangelization of an individual at a particularly vulnerable stage of life is opportunistic. Not according to the position presented in this book: that crises frequently are a product of the individual's conscious or unconscious need or desire to acquire a new identity. Of course there is a fine line between invitation and imposition, a line that Christians must respect. This is particularly important when dealing with individuals who have been in psychiatric wards and have consequently experienced continuous manipulation and coercive measures in the name of "mental health."

Since the church is recruiting soldiers for a (nonviolent) battle against evil in which time and space are severely limited, it seems legitimate to give priority to persons inclined to respond positively to Christ. However, since the church respects individuals of other faiths, it should offer asylum to them as well (e.g., Buddhists or Muslims who are experiencing a "mental breakdown"; even an Orthodox Jew is likely to prefer an asylum run by Christians to one run by those who have no inhibitions about imposing their psychiatric faith on patients.)

If this program is implemented, it will be the first time "mental patients" have the opportunity to be initiated into role identities not as "chronic mental patients" but as disciples of Christ. They will then belie the mythology of mental illness and undermine the caste system established and maintained by the mental health system at its most strategic link. This will prove that the redemptive blessings of Christianity are available even to those who are regarded as beyond salvation in the eyes of the mental health establishment.

Finally, the church should recognize that it is not "mental illness" but professionalism that is the greatest obstacle to the creation of a more humane social order. McKnight points out that with the shrinking of the manufacturing sector of the U.S. economy, by the year 2000 nearly 80 percent of the workforce in will have moved from production to the service sector. In order for the government to simultaneously increase the Gross National Product and control unemployment, it must increase the number of service sector jobs. Furthermore, the privileged groups in society (e.g., college graduates and homemakers) entering the workforce expect the prestige accorded to professional work.[19]

The real goal of the human service sector is not to ameliorate the plight of needy people but to *create* needy people. As McKnight puts it, "In business terms, the client is less the consumer than the raw material for the servicing system. . . . *His essential function is to meet the needs of servicers, the servicing system, and the national economy.*"[20] It is not that increasing numbers of the population are "mentally ill" or incompetent and in need of professional help; the truth is the very opposite. It is the professionals who need clients (who have been cultured to depend emotionally upon professionals) to provide them with a steady source of income.

Tana Dineen, a psychologist who gave up the practice of psychology in disgust, writes,

> Psychology is not the profession that it claims to be, nor is it just a business like other businesses. It is too big and too dangerous now not to be seen, and critiqued, as an industry complete with advertising slogans, sales and marketing programs, research and development, production and assembly lines, and unions. . . . With degrees in psychology, medicine, social work, nursing, or with no academic qualifications as well, the expanding workforce of the Psychology Industry relies for its survival and growth on its ability to manufacture victims.[21]

The number of psychologists has risen twentyfold since 1970, and there is an even more rapid growth of other mental health professionals.

Dineen notes further that, "Not only has supply kept up with demand, it has, in fact, exceeded it, creating the need for greater marketing of psychological services and for the development of new 'products' and the expansion of the markets for the psychology industry."[22] This endeavor, with the support of the government, has been successful. Forty-six percent of the U.S. population now report having seen a mental health professional at some point in their life, as opposed to fourteen percent in the early 1960s.[23]

The work of Laing, Szasz, Goffman and others has revealed how the mental health system transforms persons into patients. McKnight and others (e. g., Funciello, Polsky) have shown how the welfare system and the human services sector in general transforms persons into clients.[24] The result is the permanent stratification of society into competent professionals and deficient clients.

As the church campaigned against slavery as a violation of Christian ethics in the nineteenth century and against segregation in the twentieth, so today it must take a stand against professionalism as the modern form of domination. The church must unflinchingly confront the fact that promoting Christian values will be causing massive social disorganization, leaving millions of professionals without employment. It is our unwillingness to confront these facts and to work out a solution that keeps humans captive to the powers that reign in a corrupt society. It is the responsibility of the church to act as an instrument of the kingdom of God, even if this requires radical social reorganization.

This kind of radical social change requires that Christians take seriously once again the eschatological goal that was the basis of Christ's and St. Paul's mission. "So do not worry, saying, 'What shall we eat?' or 'What shall we drink?' or 'What shall we wear?' For the pagans run after all these things, and your heavenly Father knows that you need them. But seek first his kingdom and his righteousness, and all these things will be given to you as well" (Matthew 6:31-33).

This social change will occur only if there is a significant number of people who give priority to the kingdom of God and are willing to renounce policies that violate Christian norms. It also requires that Christians creatively design a social plan that can provide a livelihood—or at least welfare relief—for those middle-class professionals who presently "serve" in a parasitic mental health system that places industrial growth over social welfare.

By developing a strong democratic community on the New Testament model—one in which each member has a ministry, a gift that contributes to the common good of all and the growth of the body of Christ—the church will be striving to live in the light of the new age inaugurated by Christ and thus acting as a transformative example for the world. By creating a culture in which loving and knowing are conjoined in the act of corporate worship, the church will foster a sense of communion among individuals based on an awareness of their common creaturehood and dependence on God's benediction. By cultivating a society based on worship the church will foster the reestablishment of the communion between each human being and God, thus evoking the descent of the grace of the Holy Spirit. By nurturing a sensibility in which humans and nature are regarded as sacred icons of God, mediums for the disclosure of his majesty, the church will be resisting the corrosive secularism of modern culture which depicts human beings and nature as mere means for the pursuit of materialistic ends. And by extending the benefits of redemption to society's pariahs, the church will be attacking the unjust principle through which a corrupt oligarchy works together with a debased psychiatric priesthood in order to maintain its domination over other human beings, mask it in the pieties of modern liberal thought and reify its effects as inevitable products of nature.

The major problem that Christians confront today is how to revive the eschatological vision—the kingdom of God on earth—that animated the early Christians, that brought enemies together in the same church, that gave individuals the courage to break from the ways of the past and to take up the cross, that created the miracle of a new humanity, and that is now regarded as an outmoded relic of a prescientific age. I can only hope and pray that assuming the tasks outlined in this chapter—and in this book—will help enhance Christians' sense of what is possible so that they will realize that the kingdom of God on earth is not the anachronistic vision of ignorant, superstitious, premodern peoples but the substance of Christian faith, the ideal for which Jesus gave his life and the goal of the work of the church.

Notes

Introduction
[1]Georges Florovsky, *Bible, Church, and Tradition* (Belmont, Mass.: Nordland, 1972), pp. 70-71.
[2]It will be argued below that democracy is a direct outgrowth of Jesus' teachings and praxis.
[3]Jean Delumeau, *Sin and Fear: The Emergence of a Western Guilt Culture, 13th-18th Century* (New York: St. Martin's, 1990), p. 557.
[4]Thomas Finger, *Christian Theology: An Eschatological Approach* (Scottdale, Penn.: Herald, 1989), 2:289.

Chapter 1: The Religion of Psychiatry
[1]Thomas Szasz, *The Myth of Mental Illness* (New York: Hocher, Harpers, 1961).
[2]Ibid., pp. x-xii.
[3]Thomas Szasz, *Ideology and Insanity: Essays on the Psychiatric Dehumanization of Man* (Garden City, N.Y.: Anchor, 1970), pp. 21-24.
[4]R. D. Laing, *The Politics of Experience* (New York: Pantheon, 1967).
[5]Thomas Szasz, *The Manufacture of Madness: A Comparative Study of the Inquisition and the Mental Health Movement* (New York: Harper & Row, 1970), p. 267.
[6]Laing, *Politics of Experience,* p. 122.
[7]This term was used by family therapists to indicate that the individual who manifested the most distress reflected the dysfunctionality of the family unit as a whole.
[8]See Joel Elizur and Salvador Minuchin, *Institutionalizing Madness* (New York: Basic Books, 1989).
[9]Jay Haley, *Leaving Home: The Therapy of Disturbed Young People* (New York: McGraw-Hill, 1980).
[10]Ibid., pp. 9-47.
[11]See the account of the therapeutic asylums in Loren Mosher and Lorenzo Burti, *Community Mental Health* (New York: W. W. Norton, 1989).
[12]See also Minuchin's more recent critique of this practice: Salvador Minuchin and Michael Nichols, *Family Healing: Tales of Hope and Renewal from Family Therapy* (New York: Free Press, 1993).
[13]An account of this conference can be found in Carlos Amantea, *The Lourdes of Arizona* (San Diego: Mho & Mho, 1989).
[14]Ibid., pp. 148-49.
[15]Ibid., p. 157.
[16]Ibid., p. 150.
[17]Ibid., p. 163.
[18]R. D. Laing, *The Voice of Experience* (New York: Pantheon, 1982).
[19]Ibid., p. 51.
[20]Ibid.
[21]Ibid., p. 52.
[22]Ibid.
[23]A classic example of how mental health professionals' commitment to their theories can prevent them from making "contact" with reality was provided by David Rosenhan. In a

study he conducted "normal" human beings (professionals, lawyers, doctors with no psychiatric history) feigned insanity in order to gain admittance to several psychiatric wards. Although they acted normally once they were admitted to the ward, none of the psychiatrists or other mental health professionals suspected that they were not psychotic, despite the fact that in a number of cases the pseudopatients were subjected to long interviews by psychologists. The label so colored the professionals' perception of the "patients" that even normal behavior was interpreted as pathological. It is perhaps revealing that the only persons in the hospitals who suspected that the pseudopatients were not really patients were the other patients. When the mock patients were released from the hospital, all of their records were marked "schizophrenia in remission." See David L. Rosenhan, "On Being Sane in Insane Places," in Paul Watzlawick, *The Invented Reality* (New York: W. W. Norton, 1984), pp. 117-45.

[24]Peter Breggin, *Psychiatric Drugs: Hazards to the Brain* (New York: Springer, 1983). See also his more recent book cited below, *Toxic Psychiatry* (New York: St. Martin's Press, 1991).

[25]Seth Farber, *Madness, Heresy and the Rumor of Angels: The Revolt Against the Mental Health System* (Chicago: Open Court, 1993).

[26]A. Cua, "Basic Metaphor and the Emergence of Root Metaphors," *The Journal of Mind and Behavior* 3 (1982).

[27]Laing had argued that schizophrenia was frequently a spiritual crisis and that the breakdown could be an opportunity for a breakthrough and an existential rebirth. See Laing's *Politics of Experience.*

[28]See Northrop Frye, *Anatomy of Criticism* (Princeton, N.J.: Princeton University Press, 1973), pp. 186-206.

[29]Farber, *Madness, Heresy & the Rumor of Angels*, p. 27.

[30]It is difficult to give an "objective," as opposed to a culturally relative, definition of *madness* in an age in which prominent philosophers deny that there is an "objective reality." Nevertheless I would maintain that the "mad" individual is in an "altered state of consciousness" such that phenomena in the "real world" appear and act as they would in a dream or under the influence of hallucinogenic drugs. The poetic-dreamlike quality of madness is illustrated by the examples in the chapter. See also the discussion of madness and mysticism in Laing, *Politics of Experience*, pp. 100-168.

[31]I do not intend to deal in this book with that small percentage of mental patients who have committed criminal offenses or who seem to have a proclivity to criminal behavior. That is an entirely different subject.

[32]Michel Foucault, *Madness and Civilization: A History of Insanity in the Age of Reason* (New York: Random House, 1965), p. x.

[33]Richard Rorty, *Philosophy and the Mirror of Nature* (Princeton, New Jersey: Princeton University Press, 1979), p. 360.

Chapter 2: Psychiatry's Invasion of Family & Community Life

[1]Joe Sharkey, *Bedlam: Greed, Profiteering & Fraud in a Mental Health System Gone Crazy* (New York: St. Martin's, 1994).

[2]Testimony before the U.S. House of Representatives Select Committee on Children, Youth and Families regarding fraudulent practices in the mental health professions. *Congressional Record*, April 28, 1992.

[3]Sharkey, *Bedlam*, p. 11.

[4]Ibid., p. 186.

[5]Ibid., p. 96.

[6]Ibid., p. 90.

[7]*American Medical News*, cited in Seth Farber, "The Bedlamming of America," *Liberty* 8 (December 1994): 35.

[8]Sharkey, *Bedlam*, p. 93.

[9]Testimony before the U.S. House of Representatives Select Committee on Children, Youth and Families regarding fraudulent practices in the mental health professions. *Congressional Record*, April 28, 1992.

[10]Sharkey, *Bedlam*, p. 93.

[11]New York Commission on Quality Care for the Mentally Disabled, cited in Farber, "Bedlamming of America," p. 35.

[12]Jim Kent, cited in Farber, "Bedlamming of America," p. 35.

[13]Ira Schwartz, cited in Sharkey, *Bedlam*, p. 105.

[14]Ibid., p. 128.

[15]Ibid.

[16]Curtis Decker, cited in Sharkey, *Bedlam*, p. 129.

[17]At that time I had had over fifteen years' experience as a psychotherapist. I had completed my doctorate in psychology in 1984 and had spent several years in postgraduate training in family therapy. I was the founder of the Network Against Coercive Psychiatry and the author of *Madness, Heresy and the Rumor of Angels: The Revolt Against the Mental Health System* (Chicago: Open Court, 1993).

[18]The DSM III R (now replaced by the DSM IV), the Bible of mental health professionals, is a compendium of diagnoses. One or more of these diagnoses must be ascribed to the patient in order to receive reimbursement from insurance companies and to justify psychiatric treatment.

[19]Peter Breggin and Ginger Breggin, *The War Against Children* (New York: St. Martin's, 1994), p. 74.

[20]Gerald Coles, *The Learning Mystique: A Critical Look at Learning Disabilities* (New York: Pantheon, 1987), p. 23.

[21]Ibid., p. 205.

[22]Richard Vatz, "Attention Deficit Delirium," *Wall Street Journal*, July 27, 1994.

[23]Ibid.

[24]Fred Baughman, letter to the editor, *New York Times*, April 12, 1995.

[25]Diane McGuinness, "Attention Deficit Disorder: The Emperor's New Clothes, Animal 'Pharm' and Other Fictions," in *The Limits of Biological Treatments for Psychological Distress*, ed. S. Fisher and R. Greenberg (Hillside, N.J.: Lawrence Erlbaum, 1989).

[26]Ibid., p. 151.

[27]Ibid., p. 155.

[28]Ibid., p. 167.

[29]Peter Schrag and Diane Divoky, *The Myth of the Hyperactive Child and Other Means of Child Control* (New York: Pantheon, 1975), p. xv.

[30]John Holt, cited in Peter Breggin, *Toxic Psychiatry* (New York: St. Martin's, 1991), p. 313.

[31]McGuinness, "Attention Deficit Disorder," p. 170.

[32]John Gatto, *The Exhausted School* (New York: Oxford Village Press, 1993), p. 109.

[33]John Gatto, "I May Be a Teacher, but I'm not an Educator" (New York, flier); see also John Gatto, *Dumbing Us Down* (Philadelphia: New Society, 1992).

[34]John Merrow, "Reading, Writing and Ritalin," *New York Times*, October 21, 1995, Op-Ed..

[35]McGuinness, "Attention Deficit Disorder," p. 173.

[36]Ibid., pp. 179-80.

[37]National Institute of Mental Health, cited in Breggin and Breggin, *War Against Children*, p. 84.

[38]Breggin and Breggin, *War Against Children*, p. 85.

[39]Ibid., p. 86.

[40]Melton Schwartz, cited in Sandra Goodman, "Shock Therapy: It's Back," *Washington Post*, September 24, 1996, p. 14.

[41]For this kind of analysis see Seth Farber, "Romancing Electroshock," *Z*, June 1991, pp. 92-99.

[42]Modified ECT (the "new" ECT) differs from unmodified (the "old" ECT) in several respects: the patient is given a sedative (several hours before treatment), a muscle paralyzer and a general anesthetic. The patient is also artificially respirated with oxygen. The purpose of these modifications was not, as some advocates claim, to reduce memory loss and brain damage but to prevent fractures from the severe muscle spasms that the unmodified ECT caused. Breggin argues that "the new procedure is actually more harmful, among other reasons because the modifications raise the seizure threshold, making it necessary to increase the intensity of electricity applied to the brain." See Peter Breggin, *Brain Disabling Treatments in Psychiatry* (New York: Springer, 1997), p. 149.

[43]Peter Breggin, "The Return of ECT," *Readings in American Ortho-Psychiatry Association 7*, no. 1 (1992): 13.

[44]*The Practice of Electro-Convulsive Therapy: Recommendations for Treatment, Training and Privileging* (Washington, D.C.: American Psychiatric Association, 1990).

[45]Melton Schwartz, cited in Goodman, "Shock Therapy," p. 18.

[46]Breggin, *Brain Disabling Treatments*; see also John Friedberg, *Shock Treatment Is Not Good for Your Brain* (San Francisco: Glide, 1976).

[47]The elderly account for more than half of the estimated 100,000 individuals receiving electroshock each year—of all groups women in their seventies are the largest group of ECT recipients. Medicare picks up the bill for individuals over sixty-five and is the biggest source of reimbursement for ECT (Goodman, "Shock Therapy," p. 19). In Texas, the only state that keeps track, sixty-five-year-olds get 360% more electroshock than sixty-four-year-olds. As reporter Dennis Couchon succinctly explains, "The difference: Medicare pays." (*USA Today*, December 6, 1995, cover story.) In California the percentage of patients over sixty-five being shocked increased from 28.7 percent in 1977 to 53.1 percent in 1988 (Breggin, *Toxic Psychiatry*, p. 193).

[48]Leonard Frank, "Electroshock: Death, Brain Damage, Memory Loss and Brainwashing," *Challenging the Therapeutic State: Critical Perspectives on Psychiatry and the Mental Health System*, ed. David Cohen, special issue of *The Journal of Mind and Behavior* 11, nos. 3 and 4 (1990).

[49]Peter Breggin, *Electro-Shock: Its Brain Disabling Effects* (New York: Springer, 1990), p. 60.

[50]Frank, "Electroshock," p. 499.

[51]Goodman, "Shock Therapy," p. 19.

[52]David Kroessler and Barry Fogel, "Electro-Convulsive Therapy for Major Depression in the Oldest Old," *American Journal of Geriatric Psychiatry* 1, no. 1 (1993): 30-36.

[53]Evidently embarrassed by their findings, the authors attempted to explain it away by claiming that those patients who had been assigned to the ECT treatment had been medically sicker than the patients assigned to the non-ECT treatment. They present no data to corroborate this claim, which seems to fly in the face of common sense: one would expect doctors would be *less* likely to prescribe electro-shock for physically ill older patients.

[54]Mark Smith, "Electroshock Treatment," *Houston Chronicle*, March 8, 1992, p. 11.

[55]Dennis Cauchon, "Shock Therapy: Treatments Are Rising and Elderly Most At Risk" *USA Today*, December 6, 1995, p. 60.

[56]Peter Breggin, cited in Farber, "Romancing Electroshock," pp. 97-98.

[57]See R. Kessler, et al., "Lifetime and Month Prevalence of the DSM 3R Disorders in the United States: Results from the National Co-Morbidity Survey," *Archives of General Psychiatry* 1 (January 1994): 8-19.

[58]Ibid., pp. 8, 10 (emphasis added).

[59]Shortly after this publication President Clinton agreed to increase funding to the mental health professions as part of his proposed general health care plan.

[60]L. J. Davis, "The Encyclopedia of Insanity," *Harper's*, February 1997, p. 61.

[61]Ibid., pp. 61-66.

[62]Sharkey, *Bedlam*, pp. 284-85.

[63]Ibid., p. 283.

[64]David Cohen, ed., *Challenging the Therapeutic State: Critical Perspectives on Psychiatry and the Mental Health System*, special issue of *Journal of Mind and Behavior* 11, nos. 3 and 4 (1990), preface.

[65]Ibid.

[66]Ibid.

[67]David Cohen, ed., *Challenging the Therapeutic State: Critical Perspectives on Psychiatry and the Mental Health System*, pt. 2, special issue of *The Journal of Mind and Behavior* 15, nos. 1 and 2 (1994), preface.

[68]Ibid.

[69]See Thomas Kuhn, *The Structure of Scientific Revolutions* (Chicago: University of Chicago Press, 1970); and Richard Bernstein, *Beyond Objectivism and Relativism* (Philadelphia: University of Pennsylvania Press, 1983).

Chapter 3: The Christian Revolution & Its Legacy

[1]R. D. Laing, *The Politics of Experience* (New York: Pantheon, 1967), pp. 11-12.

[2]R. D. Laing, cited in Carlos Amantea, *The Lourdes of Arizona* (San Diego: Mho & Mho, 1989), p. 149.

[3]Laing was not at all sympathetic to Communism; rather he doubted the ostensible idealism of the U.S. government's motives, considering the fact that the overwhelming majority of victims were defenseless civilians.

[4]R. D. Laing, *Politics of Experience*, p. 76.

[5]Ibid., p. 77.

[6]Ibid., p. 94.

[7]Laing's account, given at the conference in Phoenix.

[8]R. D. Laing, *Wisdom, Madness and Folly: The Making of a Psychiatrist* (New York: McGraw Hill, 1985), p. 28.

[9]Ibid., p. 29.

[10]Ibid.

[11]Ibid., pp. 29-30.

[12]R. D. Laing, cited in Amantea, *Lourdes of Arizona*, p. 156.

[13]R. D. Laing, *Politics of Experience*, p. 143.

[14]Ibid.

[15]Ibid., p. 133.

[16]Ibid., p. 120.

[17]Thomas Szasz, *Schizophrenia: The Sacred Symbol of Psychiatry* (Syracuse, N.Y.: Syracuse University Press, 1988). Szasz characterizes Laing as a dictatorial Marxist sympathetic to the Soviet Union. Since this misperception may have biased Szasz's reading of Laing, it is worth commenting upon. Laing was a strong critic of the war in Vietnam, and he identified

in the 1960s with some of the ideals of the New Left. However, if one reads all of his books—without deeming him guilty by dint of his association with psychiatrist and Maoist David Cooper—it is clear that his critique of Western society includes communist societies as well as capitalist. Furthermore, it is evident from statements that Laing made in the 1970s and 1980s that he regarded Western democracies (with all their undemocratic tendencies) as lesser evils compared to the communist tyrannies that existed in the Soviet bloc and in China.

[18]Ibid., p. 285.

[19]Although Laing's original experiment was not very successful (for reasons that have to do with factors extraneous to his theory) Laingian-inspired crisis centers in the United States were very successful before they closed for lack of funding. See Daniel Burston, *The Wing of Madness: The Life and Work of R. D. Laing* (Cambridge, Mass.: Harvard University Press, 1996).

[20]Szasz tries to avoid using the term *deviant* because it carries "an implication of inferiority" (Thomas Szasz, *The Manufacture of Madness: A Comparative Study of the Inquisition and the Mental Health Movement* [New York: Harper & Row, 1970], p. xxv). I want to emphasize that I am in entire agreement with Szasz's contention that the chronicity of "schizophrenia" is in large part an artifact of the practices of the mental health profession.

[21]Ibid.

[22]Ibid., p. 267.

[23]Ibid., p. 271.

[24]Ibid., p. 279.

[25]Ibid., p. 268.

[26]Ibid., pp. 286-87.

[27]Ibid., p. 285.

[28]Ibid.

[29]Gustaf Aulén, *Christus Victor* (New York: Macmillan, 1969).

[30]Hendrik Berkhof, *Christ and the Powers,* trans. John H. Yoder (Scottdale, Penn.: Herald, 1977), p. 38.

[31]Thomas Finger, *Christian Theology: An Eschatological Approach* (Scottdale, Penn.: Herald, 1989), 2:329.

[32]Berkhof, *Christ and the Powers,* p. 39.

[33]Girard was born in France in 1923 and emigrated to the United States in 1947. After many years of teaching literature and language at universities, Girard underwent a conversion to the Christian faith in 1959. He is now professor emeritus of French language, literature and civilization at Stanford University.

[34]See René Girard, *Things Hidden Since the Foundation of the World* (Stanford, Calif.: Stanford University Press, 1978).

[35]James Alison, *Raising Abel* (New York: Crossroad, 1996), p. 114.

[36]Girard, *Things Hidden Since the Foundation of the World,* p. 164.

[37]René Girard, *The Girard Reader,* ed. James G. Williams (New York: Crossroad, 1996), p. 201.

[38]René Girard, *The Scapegoat* (Baltimore, Md.: John Hopkins University Press, 1986), p. 189.

[39]Ibid.

[40]Ibid., p. 190.

[41]Ibid., p. 207.

[42]Girard, *Girard Reader,* pp. 208-9.

[43]Elisabeth Schüssler Fiorenza, *In Memory of Her* (New York: Crossroad, 1983), p. 148.

[44]Clement of Alexandria, cited in Elaine Pagels, *Adam, Eve and the Serpent* (New York:

Random House, 1988), p. 39.

[45]Harry Jaffa, *The New Birth of Freedom* (forthcoming).

[46]Ibid., p. 39.

[47]Theodore Parker, *Discourses of Politcs*, vol. 4, *The Collected Works of Theodore Parker*, ed. Frances Power Cobbe (London: Trübner, 1863-1865), p. 267.

[48]Gordon Wood, *The Radicalism of the American Revolution* (New York: Alfred Knopf, 1992), p. 235.

[49]Girard, *Girard Reader*, p. 201.

[50]Judi Chamberlin, "The Ex-Patients Movement," *Challenging the Therapeutic State: Critical Perspectives on Psychiatry and the Mental Health System*, ed. David Cohen, special issue of *The Journal of Mind and Behavior* 2, nos. 3 and 4 (1990): 333.

[51]See Robyn Dawes, *House of Cards; Psychology and Psycho-Therapy Built on Myth* (New York: Free Press, 1994), pp. 90-91.

[52]Since psychology constitutes a religion, the government's mandating of psychiatric incarceration as well as outpatient counseling is a violation of individuals' religious freedom as well as the separation of church and state.

[53]Frederick Douglass, cited in Szasz, *Manufacture of Madness*, p. 289.

[54]I started this chapter by examining some of the ways—as seen by Laing and Szasz—in which society is incongruent with Christian values and thus ought not to be taken as normative in assessing spiritual well-being, or "mental health." I then qualified my conclusion by showing that over the centuries Christian values have had some positive effect on society. But the Christianization, or democratization, of society has only gone so far and has now seemingly come to an impasse. I will argue in this book that the spiritual-social crisis which confronts us now is so profound that if we are to survive as a species, the church must act as an agent of social and spiritual transformation, thus assuming responsibilities it has shirked—out of timidity, mendacity or opportunism—for far too long.

Chapter 4: The Challenge to the Church

[1]*Radical Reformation* refers to those Christian denominations that generally supported the Reformation but broke from it when its continued coalition with the state clearly was leading to the compromise of Christian principles. See John Howard Yoder, *The Priestly Kingdom* (Notre Dame, Ind.: University of Notre Dame Press, 1984).

[2]John Howard Yoder, *The Royal Priesthood* (Grand Rapids, Mich.: Eerdmans, 1994), p. 80.

[3]John Howard Yoder, cited in Rodney Clapp, *A Peculiar People* (Downers Grove, Ill.: InterVarsity Press, 1997), p. 28. Luther made the classic distinction between the visible (earthly) and the invisible (spiritual) church. He argued that the former is necessarily a distorted actualization of the latter.

[4]Let me be clear: I am not denying that our salvation is dependent on the grace of God; I am merely affirming—in accordance with my reading of the Bible—that God demands our cooperation in the work of salvation.

[5]Why Eastern theology, as opposed to Western, maintained an eschatological motif is a question beyond the compass of this book. However, I will note that at least part of the reason consists in the relatively insignificant influence of Augustine on Eastern Christianity. See Elaine Pagels, *Adam, Eve and the Serpent* (New York: Random House, 1984).

[6]N. T. Wright, *Jesus and the Victory of God* (Minneapolis: Fortress, 1996), p. 19.

[7]Albert Schweitzer, *The Quest of the Historical Jesus* (London: A & C Black, 1954).

[8]John Howard Yoder, *The Original Revolution* (Scottdale, Penn.: Herald, 1972), p. 66.

[9]Rodney Clapp, *Families at the Crossroads* (Downers Grove, Ill.: InterVarsity Press, 1993),

p. 74.

[10]While most nonevangelical mainline Protestants recognize that the kingdom of Christianity involves the struggle for social justice, they do not take the kingdom of God seriously as a political and supernatural phenomenon that can potentially determine the course and direction of history. For them too salvation is either relegated to the "other world" or it is eschewed entirely in the name of "realism." For a critique of this, see Howard Snyder, *The Community of the King* (Downers Grove, Ill.: InterVarsity Press, 1978).

[11]See the astute critique of Bultmann and his school in J. Christiaan Beker, *Paul the Apostle* (Philadelphia: Fortress, 1980), pp. 139-47.

[12]See G. C. Berkouwer, *The Return of Christ* (Grand Rapids, Mich.: Eerdmans, 1992), p. 229.

[13]Ibid., p. 226.

[14]Ibid., p. 231.

[15]J. Christiaan Beker, *Paul the Apostle: The Triumph of God in Life and Thought* (Philadelphia: Fortress, 1984), p. 356.

[16]Snyder, *Community of the King*, p. 55.

[17]Martin Buber, cited in Berkouwer, *Return of Christ*, p. 229.

[18]See the discussion of the eschatological sensibility in Charles Scriven, *The Transformation of Culture* (Scottdale, Penn.: Herald, 1988), p. 186.

[19]Wright, *Jesus and the Victory of God.*

[20]Ibid., see also, for example, pp. 286-87; 296-97.

[21]See Elisabeth Schüssler Fiorenza, *In Memory of Her* (New York: Crossroad, 1983), p. 121.

[22]Clement of Alexandria, cited in Elaine Pagels, *Adam, Eve & the Serpent* (New York: Random House, 1988), p. 51.

[23]Clapp, *A Peculiar People*, p. 166.

[24]Vladimir Lossky, *Orthodox Theology* (Crestwood, New York: St. Vladimir's Seminary Press, 1989), p. 85.

[25]Martin Buber, cited in Jürgen Moltmann, *The Theology of Hope* (Minneapolis: Fortress Press, 1993), p. 124.

[26]George Eldon Ladd, *The Presence of the Future* (Grand Rapids, Mich.: Eerdmans, 1974), pp. 321-24.

Chapter 5: The Western Shame-and-Guilt Culture & the Myth of Mental Illness

[1]Ron Leifer, *In the Name of Mental Health* (New York: Science House, 1969), pp. 36-37.

[2]In the last two decades psychiatrists have asserted that psychiatric disorders are in fact disorders of the brain, but this was not the theory that dominated psychology for most of the twentieth century.

[3]Kate Millett was already a famous author at the time she was labeled mentally ill. Despite her high status, she was devastated by the "diagnosis." In a speech given in 1990, she testified at a gathering of former "mental patients": "Remember how you had to truckle before a system which has caused you to suffer and humiliated you nearly to death? What do I remember of that time?"

> When I lost my mind to the extent that I believed the nonsense of the medical model, that I was mentally ill, bent my head before unreason, saw myself as the others saw me, as the system saw me, disappeared to myself, expired, vanished as a point of view. I remember this: a sense of the inexplicable in my fate, destiny, sense of doom, helplessness. The fault lay in my mind. . . . You knelt down, you capitulated, you said uncle, you swallowed your pride and your selfhood, you bit the bullet and took the pill. . . . It was death in life, a half-life, a bondage of the mind in several ways—the mind befuddled with drugs, the mind no longer believed in

or trusted. After all, faith in one's own perceptions is one's definition of integrity and wholeness. That was lost. Saddest of all was one's own intellectual honor, its loss."

After over ten years Millett finally rejected her official diagnosis of "manic-depressive" and stopped taking psychiatric drugs. She has now been off "medication" for over ten years. Cited in Seth Farber, *Madness, Heresy and the Rumor of Angels: The Revolt Against the Mental Health System* (Chicago: Open Court, 1993), p. 254.

[4]Dogma that "mental disorders" are caused by traumatic events in the first several years of life is belied by considerable data. Both Kenneth Gergen and Jerome Kagan agree that behavior patterns in the first six years of life have virtually no predictable validity in relation to behavior shown during adulthood. See the discussion in Seth Farber, "Institution of Mental Health and Social Control," *Challenging the Therapeutic State: Critical Perspectives on Psychiatry and the Mental Health System*, ed. David Cohen, special issue of *The Journal of Mind and Behavior* 11, nos. 3 and 4 (1990).

Gergen's work bears out my own contention, made repeatedly throughout this book, that development is fundamentally idiosyncratic. He writes, "The individual seems fundamentally flexible in most aspects of personal functioning. Significant change in the life course may occur at any time. . . . An immense panoply of developmental forms seems possible; which particular form emerges may depend on a confluence of particulars, the existence of which is fundamentally unsystematic." Kenneth Gergen, "The Emerging Crisis in Life-Span Developmental Theory," in *Life-Span, Development and Behavior,* ed. P. Baltes and O. Brim (New York: Academic Press, 1980), p. 43.

[5]For a more detailed discussion of this see Seth Farber, *Eternal Day: The Christian Alternative to Secularism and Modern Psychology* (Salisbury, Mass.: Regina Orthodox Press, 1998).

[6]For a Christian critique of this see Clark Pinnock, ed., *The Grace of God and the Will of Man* (Minneapolis: Bethany House, 1989); and Clark Pinnock and Robert Brow, *Unbounded Love* (Downers Grove, Ill.: InterVarsity Press, 1994).

[7]See Jean Delumeau, *Sin and Fear: The Emergence of a Western Guilt Culture, 13th-18th Century* (New York: St. Martin's, 1990), pp. 246-82; and Jaroslav Pelikan, *The Emergence of the Catholic Tradition: 100-600* (Chicago: University of Chicago Press, 1971), pp. 298-304.

[8]Augustine, cited in Elaine Pagels, *Adam, Eve and the Serpent* (New York: Random House, 1988), p. 109.

[9]Ibid., p. 113.

[10]Clark Pinnock, *Tracking the Maze* (San Francisco: Harper & Row, 1990), p. 192.

[11]For an explanation of this see Farber, *Eternal Day.*

[12]Delumeau, *Sin and Fear,* p. 248.

[13]Ibid., p. 296.

[14]Ibid., p. 298.

[15]David Cohen, "The Biological Basis of Schizophrenia: The Evidence Reconsidered," *Social Work* (May 1989), pp. 255-57.

[16]Ibid., p. 256.

[17]See for example Theodore Sarbin, "Toward the Obsolescence of the Schizophrenia Hypothesis," *Challenging the Therapeutic State: Critical Perspectives on Psychology and the Mental Health System*, ed. David Cohen, special issue of *Journal of Mind and Behavior* 11, nos. 3 and 4 (1990): 259-83; and Farber, *Madness, Heresy and the Rumor of Angels.*

[18]Peter Breggin, *Toxic Psychiatry* (New York: St. Martin's, 1991), p. 354.

[19]Ibid.

[20]Ibid., pp. 354-55.

[21]See Farber, *Eternal Day.*

[22]In a distant epoch children were viewed essentially as defective adults, but childhood is now regarded as a natural state. See John Sommerville, *The Rise and Fall of Childhood* (Beverly Hills, Calif.: Sage, 1982), pp. 47-49; and Philippe Ariès, *Centuries of Childhood* (New York: Vintage, 1962).

[23]I am not arguing that physical illness should be redefined as growth but rather that the phenomenon termed *mental illness* is vastly different; that the resolution of these problems is impeded by the theories and practices of mental health professionals.

[24]The reverence with which children are held in this culture (they are frequently described as "precious") may be said to be implicitly if not explicitly sacramental. They are often treated (as adults rarely are) as icons of God who manifest his purity and innocence.

[25]Father Alexander Schmemann wrote, "Perhaps the greatest tragedy of our recent history is the fact that the most Christian of all ideas in our world, that of the absolute value of human personality, has been raised and defended historically in opposition to the Church community and has become a powerful symbol of the struggle against the Church." Alexander Schmemann, *Historical Road of Eastern Orthodoxy* (Crestwood, N.Y.: St. Vladimir's Seminary Press, 1963), p. 58.

[26]For an elaboration on this point, see Farber, *Eternal Day.*

[27]Jim Owen, *Christian Psychology's War on God's Word* (Santa Barbara, Calif.: East Gate, 1993), p. 79.

[28]Pinnock and Brow, *Unbounded Love,* p. 10.

[29]Ibid., p. 28.

[30]John Stott, *The Cross of Christ* (Downers Grove, Ill.: InterVarsity Press, 1986), p. 282.

[31]S. L. Frank, *Reality and Man* (London: Faber & Faber, 1965), pp. 122-23.

[32]Philip Sherrard, *Christianity and Eros* (London: SPCK, 1976), p. 47.

[33]Philip Sherrard, *Human Image* (Edinburgh: Golgonooza, 1992), p. 173.

[34]Alexander Schmemann, *Church, World, Mission* (Crestwood, N.Y.: St. Vladimir's Seminary Press, 1988), p. 152.

[35]Ibid., p. 156.

[36]Alexander Schmemann, *For the Life of the World* (Crestwood, N.Y.: St. Vladimir's Seminary Press, 1988), p 111.

[37]Ibid., p. 112.

[38]S. L. Frank, *Reality and Man* (London: Faber & Faber, 1965), p. 220.

[39]Craig Dykstra, cited in Rodney Clapp, *A Peculiar People* (Downers Grove, Ill.: InterVarsity Press, 1997), p. 99.

Chapter 6: The Church as Counterculture

[1]Ron Leifer, "The Medical Model as Ideology," *Challenging the Therapeutic State: Critical Perspectives on Psychiatry and the Mental Health System,* ed. David Cohen, special issue of *The Journal of Mind and Behavior* 11, nos. 3 and 4 (1990): 250.

[2]Stanley Hauerwas and William H. Willimon, *Resident Aliens* (Nashville: Abingdon, 1989), p. 38.

[3]Ibid.

[4]Rodney Clapp, *A Peculiar People* (Downers Grove, Ill.: InterVarsity Press, 1997), p. 65.

[5]John Howard Yoder, *The Politics of Jesus* (Grand Rapids, Mich.: Eerdmans, 1972), p. 154.

[6]Charles Scriven, *The Transformation of Culture* (Scottdale, Penn.: Herald, 1988), p. 181.

[7]J. Christiaan Beker, *Paul the Apostle: The Triumph of God in Life and Thought* (Philadelphia: Fortress, 1980), pp. 318-19.

[8]Thomas Finger, *Christian Theology: An Eschatological Approach* (Scottdale, Penn.: Herald, 1987), 2:287.

[9]Ibid., p. 289.

[10]Ibid., p. 294.

[11]Ibid., p. 277.

[12]Ibid., p. 294.

[13]It is important to note that the word *clinical* in this context has no substantive meaning. Mental health professionals use it to assert in disguise what they regard as their prerogatives. Thus if an individual is suffering from a "clinical depression," he clearly needs to be seen by a professional. While this usage implies that there are ordinary "nonclinical" depressions, I have never heard a mental health professional speak of one.

[14]M. L. Smith and G. V. Glass, "Meta-analysis of Psychotherapy Outcome Studies," *American Psychologist* 32 (1977): 752-60.

[15]Robyn Dawes, *House of Cards* (New York: Macmillan, 1994), p. 54.

[16]Jerome Frank, cited in Martin Bobgan and Deirdre Bobgan, *Psychoheresy:The Psychological Seduction of Christianity* (Santa Monica, Calif.: EastGate, 1987), p. 180.

[17]Morrise Parloff, cited in Bobgan and Bobgan, *Psychoheresy*, p. 183.

[18]Bobgan and Bobgan, *Psychoheresy*, p. 187.

[19]Ibid., p. 102.

[20]Ibid., p. 104.

[21]Ibid., p. 110.

[22]Bob Passantino and Gretchen Passantino, "Pscyhology and the Church," *Christian Research Journal*, winter 1995, p. 21.

[23]N. T. Wright, *Jesus and the Victory of God* (Minneapolis: Fortress, 1996), p. 274.

[24]Ibid., p. 272.

[25]Clapp, *Peculiar People*, p. 112.

[26]R. D. Laing, *The Politics of Experience* (New York: Pantheon, 1971), p. 120.

[27]An important indication of the incompatibility of the Christian mission with the operations of the mental health system is the practice in mental hospitals of making religion a taboo. (I have been told about this by hundreds of expatients.) A patient's preoccupation with religion is said by psychiatrists to be part of his or her "illness." Accordingly, patients are discouraged from talking about religious issues or praying. In many cases Bibles are literally taken out of their hands.

Chapter 7: The Mental Patient as Exile & as Christian Initiate

[1]Szasz has characterized the modern age as the age of science and has argued that the medical doctor is a primary symbol of security (as the pope once was) and the mental patient as a symbol of insecurity (as the heretic used to be). See Thomas Szasz, *The Manufacture of Madness* (New York: Harper & Row, 1970), pp. 268-69. I would agree with Szasz and argue further that in the narrative authored by the mental health establishment, the psychiatrist as the agent of reason and order seeks to subdue, conquer and cure the lunatic as the embodiment of irrationality and disorder. (Thus the psychiatrist needs the schizophrenic— for his identity, indeed for his very existence. This is why Szasz has termed "schizophrenia" the "sacred symbol" of psychiatry.) The public views the mental patient as a threat, a symbol of insecurity, and the psychiatrist as a symbol of authority who exorcises this threat. This analysis is supported by the fact that many of the problems that afflict society today are often attributed to mental illness. For example, it is frequently alleged in the press that mental illness is the cause of homelessness and that increasing the power of the psychiatric establishment will solve this problem.

[2]Theodore Sarbin and Jay Mancuso, *Schizophrenia: Medical Diagnosis or Moral Verdict?* (New York: Pergamon, 1980).

[3]Erving Goffman, *Asylums: Essays on the Social Situation of Mental Patients and Other Inmates* (New York: Doubleday, 1961).

[4]R. D. Laing, "Evolution of Psychotherapy" (paper presented at conference sponsored by Milton H. Erickson Foundation, Phoenix, Arizona, 1985).

[5]I qualify my contention with the phrase "in large part" because I am aware that there may be some individuals who even if given the best treatment are not able to adjust to the world *as it is.* However, as I hope to show in this text, making this presumption in advance is dangerous and leads to a self-fulfilling prophecy.

[6]Jerome Frank, *Persuasion in Healing* (New York: Schocken, 1974), p. 127.

[7]Jay Haley, *Leaving Home* (New York: McGraw Hill, 1980), p. 22.

[8]Frank, *Persuasion in Healing*, pp. 127-28.

[9]Szasz, *Manufacture of Madness*, p. 267.

[10]See Seth Farber, *Madness, Heresy and the Rumor of Angels: The Revolt Against the Mental Health System* (Chicago: Open Court, 1993); and John McKnight, *The Careless Society: Community and Its Counterfeits* (New York: BasicBooks, 1995).

[11]See Rael Jean Isaac and Virginia Armat, *Madness in the Streets: How Psychiatry and the Law Abandoned the Mentally Ill* (New York: Free Press, 1990); and Myron Magnate, *The Dream and the Nighmare* (New York: William Morrow, 1993).

[12]Ann Braden Johnson, *Out of Bedlam: The Truth about Deinstitutionalization* (New York: BasicBooks, 1990), p xxii. Johnson adroitly debunks the various myths about deinstitutionalization.

[13]Andrew Scull, "Deinstitutionalization: Cycles of Despair," *Challenging the Therapeutic State: Critical Perspectives on Psychiatry and the Mental Health System,* ed. David Cohen, special issue of *The Journal of Mind and Behavior* 11, nos. 3 and 4 (1990): 247.

[14]Johnson, *Out of Bedlam,* p. 39.

[15]See Scull, "Deinstitutionalization," p. 307.

[16]Thomas Szasz, *Cruel Compassion: Psychiatry's Control of Society's Unwanted* (New York: John Wiley, 1994), p. 171.

[17]Scull, "Deinstitutionalization," p. 307.

[18]Andrew Scull, *Decarceration: Community Treatment and the Deviant* (New Brunswick, N.J.: Rutgers University Press, 1984), cited in Farber, *Madness, Heresy and the Rumor of Angels,* p. 247.

[19]John McKnight, *The Careless Society: Community and its Counterfeits* (New York: BasicBooks, 1995). McKnight states that these institutions "are places where people live wholly surrounded by service professionals, programs and plans" (p. 108).

[20]B. Alper, cited by Scull, "Deinstitutionalization," p. 307.

[21]Isaac and Armat, *Madness in the Streets.*

[22]Ibid., p. 6.

[23]Ibid., p. 222.

[24]See Seth Farber, "Undermining Community," *Telos,* winter 1995, p. 187.

[25]Thomas Szasz, "Law and Psychiatry," *Challenging the Therapeutic State: Critical Perspectives on Psychiatry and the Mental Health System,* ed. David Cohen, special issue of *The Journal of Mind and Behavior* 11, nos. 3 and 4 (1990): 561.

[26]Warren Burger, cited in Seth Farber, "The Bedlamming of America," *Liberty* 8 (December 1994): 37.

[27]Ibid.

[28]Peter Breggin, "Brain Damage and Persistent Cognitive Dysfunction Associated with Neuroleptic Drugs," *Challenging the Therapeutic State: Critical Perspectives on Psychiatry and the Mental Health System,* ed. David Cohen, special issue of *The Journal of Mind and*

Behavior 11, nos. 3 and 4 (1990): 444; and D. E. Sternberg, "Neuroleptic Malignant
Syndrome," *American Journal of Psychiatry* 143 (1986): 1273-75.

[29]*Tardive Dyskinesia: A Task Force Report of the American Psychiatric Association* (Washington,
D.C.: American Psychiatric Association, 1992).

[30]Ibid., pp. 63-64. This study also ruled out the possibility of causes of TD other than drug
treatment.

[31]Breggin, "Brain Damage and Persistent Cognitive Dysfunction," p. 429.

[32]Jack Henry Abbott, cited in John Modrow, *How To Become a Schizophrenic: The Case Against
Biological Psychiatry* (Everett, Washington: Apollyon, 1992), p. 191.

[33]Heinz Lehmann and G. E. Hanrahan, "Chlorpromazine: A New Inhibiting Agent for
Psychomotor Excitation," *Archives of Neurological Psychiatry* 71 (1954): 227-37.

[34]Heinz Lehmann, cited in Peter Breggin, *Psychiatric Drugs: Hazards to the Brain* (New York:
Springer, 1983), p. 15.

[35]Anton Stephens, cited in Breggin, *Psychiatric Drugs*, p. 15.

[36]See discussion in Breggin, *Psychiatric Drugs*, pp. 12-33.

[37]Ibid., p. 18.

[38]Peter Sterling, cited in Breggin, *Toxic Psychiatry* (New York: St. Martin's Press, 1991), p. 56.

[39]Breggin, *Psychiatric Drugs*, p. 2.

[40]David Cohen and Michael McCubbin, "The Political Economy of Tardive Dyskinesia,"
*Challenging the Therapeutic State: Critical Perspectives on Psychiatry and the Mental Health
System,* ed. David Cohen, special issue *of The Journal of Mind and Behavior* 11, nos. 3 and
4 (1990): 466-67.

[41]Ibid., p. 473. My own experience talking to hundreds of institutionalized patients confirms
this fact.

[42]*Tardive Dyskinesia*, p. 244.

[43]David Cohen, ed., "Neuroleptic Drug Treatment of Schizophrenia: The State of Confusion,"
*Challenging the Therapeutic State: Critical Perspectives on Psychiatry and the Mental Health
System,* ed. David Cohen, pt. 2, special issue of *The Journal of Mind and Behavior* 15, nos.
1 and 2 (1994): 143.

[44]See also Cohen, "Neuroleptic Drug Treatment," p. 143.

[45]Cohen and McCubbin, "Political Economy," pp. 468-69.

[46]David Cohen, "Neuroleptic Drug Treatment," p. 144.

[47]Farber, *Madness, Heresy and the Rumor of Angels.*

[48]R. D. Laing, *The Politics of Experience* (New York: Pantheon, 1967), p. 133.

[49]Ibid., pp. 144-45.

[50]Julian Silverman, "Shamans and Acute Schizophrenia," *American Anthropologist* 69 (1967):
21.

[51]Ibid.

[52]Mircea Eliade, *Myths, Dreams and Mysteries* (New York: Harper & Row, 1975), pp. 225-26.

[53]Ibid., p. 224.

[54]Ibid.

Chapter 8: The Restoration of the Authority of the Church

[1]William Shambra, "By the People," *Policy Review,* summer 1994, p. 32.

[2]Ibid.

[3]Christopher Lasch, *The Revolt of the Elites and the Betrayal of Democracy* (New York: W. W.
Norton, 1995), p. 58.

[4]Ibid., p. 79.

[5]Ibid., p. 211.

[6]James Hillman, "The Rainmaker Phantasy," *Family Therapy Networker* 15, no. 5 (1991): 64.

[7]Wendy Kaminer, *I'm Dysfunctional, You're Dysfunctional* (New York: Addison-Wesley, 1992), pp. 152, 154.

[8]Paul Piccone, "Rethinking Federalism," *Telos* 100 (summer 1994): 6.

[9]Paul Piccone, "Confronting the French New Right," *Telos* 98 and 99 (winter 1993 and spring 1994).

[10]Constance Seligman, cited in Tana Dineen, *Manufacturing Victims: What the Psychology Industry is Doing to People* (Toronto: Robert Davies, 1996), p. 238.

[11]John McKnight, *The Careless Society: Community and its Counterfeits* (New York: BasicBooks, 1995), p. 98.

[12]Ibid., p. 61.

[13]Ibid., p. 168.

[14]Ibid., p. 62.

[15]Ibid., p. 118.

[16]Ibid., p. 169.

[17]Martin Bobgan and Deirdre Bobgan, *Against Biblical Counseling: For the Bible* (Santa Monica, Calif.: East Gate, 1994), pp. 89-90.

[18]Ibid., p. 90.

[19]McKnight, *Careless Society,* p. 22.

[21]Ibid., p. 40 (emphasis added).

[21]Dineen, *Manufacturing Victims,* p. 20.

[22]Ibid., p. 19.

[23]Ibid., p. 18.

[24]See Theresa Funiciello, *The Tyranny of Kindness: Dismantling the Welfare State to End Poverty in America* (New York: Atlantic Monthly Press, 1993); and Andrew Polsky, *The Rise of the Therapeutic State* (Princeton, N.J.: Princeton University Press, 1991).

Name Index

Subject Index

no scientific foundation, 111
as religion, 149 n. 52
psychopathology, 53, 93, 95
psychotherapy, 94
psychotic delusional system, 26
Radical Reformation, 81, 106, 149 n. 1
rage reduction therapy, 39
"real world," 33-34
rebelliousness, and mental disorder, 40
recovery movement, 134
Reformation, 81
regeneration, 15, 64, 131-32
rehabilitation, 119
rehospitalization, 128
relationships, 21, 25, 27, 31, 32, 60
religious freedom, 149 n. 52
restlessness, 125
resurrection, 84-85
Ritalin, 42, 45-46
Rogerian-trained therapists, 113
Roman Empire, 75
romance, 29-30
rulers of this age, 68-70
Satan, 71, 81
scapegoating, 20, 22, 45, 65-67, 70-71, 72, 117
schizophrenia, 15, 18, 19, 20, 21-22
  as breakthrough, 144 n. 27
  chronicity of, 31, 116, 121-22, 148 n. 20
  as curable, 21, 128
  as the "sacred symbol" of psychiatry, 153 n. 1

See also mental illness
schizophrenics
  capacity for relationships, 23-25, 27, 31, 32, 60
  as defective persons, 117
  humanity of, 61
  as incurable, 94
  self-degradation, 126
  as undergoing personality crisis, 129
schools, 45, 59-60
science, 12, 19, 98, 111, 113, 136, 153 n. 1
Scriven, Charles, 108
Scull, Andrew, 118, 119
secularism, 12, 62, 101, 103, 105, 142
segregation, 141
self-confidence, 100-101
self-degradation, 126
self-denial, 103
self-discovery, 30
self-esteem, 46, 93, 120
self-respect, 30
seminaries, 112
sensitive people, 62
servanthood, 73-74
shamanism, 129-31
shyness, 53, 100
slavery, 78-79, 81, 86, 141
snobbery, 53
social justice, 86, 150 n. 10
social order, 57-59, 66
social skills, 100, 120
society, 64, 67
solitary confinement, 39
Somatics, Inc., 47-48
Soteria House, 22
spiritual growth, 29-30
spiritual life, 63

Stelazine, 35
stigmatization, 65-66
suffering, 55, 85, 99
tardive dementia, 124
tardive dyskinesia, 124, 126, 127
technique, 61
therapeutic state, 78, 133-34
Thorazine, 29, 35
tics, 46
tobacco, 48, 53
torture, 78
tranquilizers, 138
transinstitutionalization, 119
trauma, and "mental disorders," 151 n. 4
treatment-resistant patients, 124, 126, 127
United States Constitution, 76, 77, 79
victimization, 70-71, 72
video games, 53
violence, 58-59, 65, 68, 70-71
war, 58-59
welfare, 118, 134-35
Western guilt culture, 95
world
  destructive effect on church, 80
  as foolishness in God's sight, 63
  in opposition to Christ, 63, 67-68
  power of, 64
  as standard of truth, rationality and justice, 58
worship, 105, 113